+8 Thi
2 TT
1V

**Believer's
of School
Prayer**

The Believer's School of Prayer

Andrew Murray

B 831

BETHANY HOUSE PUBLISHERS
MINNEAPOLIS, MINNESOTA 55438
A Division of Bethany Fellowship, Inc.

Originally published under the title,
With Christ in the School of Prayer.

Copyright © 1982
Bethany House Publishers
All rights reserved

Published by Bethany House Publishers
A Division of Bethany Fellowship, Inc.
6820 Auto Club Road, Minneapolis, Minnesota 55438

Printed in the United States of America

Library of Congress Cataloging in Publication Data

Murray, Andrew, 1828-1917.
    The believer's school of prayer.

    (The Andrew Murray prayer library)
    Rev. ed. of: With Christ in the school of prayer.   1895.
    1. Prayer. I. Title. II. Series.
BV210.M85   1982   248.3'2   82-4401
ISBN 0-87123-195-6 (pbk.)   AACR2

The Author

ANDREW MURRAY was born in South Africa in 1828. After receiving his education in Scotland and Holland, he returned to that land and spent many years there as both pastor and missionary. He was a staunch advocate of biblical Christianity. He is best known for his many devotional books.

Other Books by Andrew Murray:

Be Perfect
The Believer's Daily Renewal
Day by Day with Andrew Murray
Holy in Christ
How to Raise Your Children for Christ
Jesus Christ: Prophet-Priest
Like Christ
The Master's Indwelling
The Ministry of Intercessory Prayer
Money
New Life
The Secret of Believing Prayer
The Spirit of Christ

Preface

Of all the promises connected with the command, "Abide in me," there is none higher, and none that sooner brings the confession, "Not that I have already attained, or am already made perfect," than this: "If ye abide in me, *ask whatsoever ye will, and it shall be done unto you.*" Power with God is the highest attainment of the life of full abiding.

Of all Christlike traits, none is higher and more glorious than conformity to Him in the work that now engages Him without ceasing in the Father's presence—His all-prevailing intercession. The more we abide in Him, and grow unto His likeness, the more will His priestly life work in us mightily and our life become what His is: a life that ever pleads and prevails for men.

"Thou hast made us kings and priests unto God." From both the king and the priest flow power, influence, blessing. In the king power comes down, in the priest, power rises and prevails with God. In our blessed Priest-King, Jesus Christ, the kingly power is founded on the priestly, *"He is able* to save to the uttermost, *because* he ever liveth to make intercession." In us, His priests and kings, this is also true. In intercession the church finds and wields its highest power. In intercession each member of the Church proves his descent from Israel, who as a prince had power with God and with men and prevailed.

This book has been written because of a deep conviction that the place and power of prayer in the Christian life is too little understood. As long as we look on prayer chiefly as the means of maintaining our own Christian life, we cannot fully know what prayer is meant to be. But when we learn to regard it as the highest part of the work entrusted to us, and as the root and strength

7

of all other work, then we shall see that there is nothing we need more than the study and practice of the art of praying in the right way.

In the progressive teaching of our Lord about prayer, and the wonderful promises on the last night (John 14:16) about the works we are to do in His name and the fruit we are to bear, one thing becomes clear. Only when the Church yields herself to this holy work of intercession can she expect the power of Christ to be manifested on her behalf. It is my prayer that God will use this book to show His children the wonderful place of power and influence He waits for them to occupy and for which a weary world also waits.

Another truth is that the Father waits to hear every prayer of faith, to give us whatsoever we will and whatsoever we ask in Jesus' name. Usually we so limit the wonderful love and the large promises of our God that we cannot read the simplest and clearest statements of our Lord without adding qualifying clauses with which to guard and expound them. The Church needs to learn that God means prayer to have an answer. Man has not yet conceived what God will do for His child who truly believes that his prayer will be heard. This truth that *God hears prayer* is universally admitted, but very few understand its full meaning or experience its power. If anyone is aroused enough to take the Master's wonderful promises simply and literally as they stand, my object in this book had been attained.

Thousands in these last years have found unspeakable blessing in learning how completely Christ is our life, how He undertakes to be and to do all in us that we need. But have we learned to apply this truth to our prayer-life? Many complain that they lack power to pray in faith, to pray the effective prayer that accomplishes much. But Jesus is waiting, is longing, to teach them this. Christ is our life. In heaven He ever lives to pray. His life in us is an ever-praying life if we only trust Him for it. Christ teaches us to pray not only by example, by instruction, by command, by promises, but *by showing us himself, the ever-living intercessor, as our life.* When we believe this and abide in Him for our prayer life too, our fears of not being able to pray aright will vanish. We shall joyfully and triumphantly trust our Lord to teach us to pray and to be himself the life and the power of our prayer.

May God open our eyes to see what the holy ministry of intercession is to which we, as His royal priesthood, have been set apart. May He help us to believe what mighty influence our prayers can exert. May all fear of being unable to fulfill our calling vanish as we see Jesus living ever in us to pray, and standing surety for our prayer life.

Andrew Murray
Wellington,
October 28, 1885

Contents

LESSON ONE

The Only Teacher

"And it came to pass, that, as he was praying in a certain place, when he ceased, one of his disciples said unto him, Lord, teach us to pray" (Luke 11:1).

The disciples had been with Christ and had seen Him pray. They had learned to understand something of the connection between His wonderful life in public and His secret life of prayer. They had learned to believe in Him as a Master in the art of prayer—none could pray like Him. So they came to Him with the request, "Lord, teach us to pray." In later years they would have told us that few things surpassed what He taught them in His lessons on prayer.

Now as He prays the watching disciples feel the need of repeating the same request, "Lord, teach us to pray." As we grow in the Christian life, the thought and the faith of Christ's never-failing intercession becomes increasingly wonderful. It arouses in us a desire to be *like Christ* in His intercession.

As we see Him pray and we remember that no one can pray or teach like Him, we agree with the disciples, "Lord, teach us to pray." As we think how all He is and has, how He himself is our very own, how He himself is our life, we feel assured that we have but to ask and He will be delighted to take us up into closer fellowship with himself and teach us to pray even as He prays.

Let us this very day say to the Master, as they did of old, "Lord, teach us to pray." As we meditate we shall find each word of our petition full of meaning.

"Lord, teach us *to pray*" is what we need to be taught. Though in its beginnings prayer is so simple that even a small child can pray, yet it is at the same time the highest and holiest work to which man can rise. It is fellowship with the unseen and most holy One. The powers of the eternal world have been placed at its disposal. It is the very essence of the true religion. It is the channel of all blessings and the secret of power and life. Through prayer God has given to all the right to take hold of Him and His strength. It is on prayer that promises wait for their fulfillment, the kingdom for its coming, the glory of God for its full revelation.

But how slothful and unfit we are for this blessed work. Only the Spirit of God can enable us to do it as it should be done. How quickly we are deceived into resting in the form while the power is missing. Our early training, the teaching of the Church, the influence of habit, the stirring of the emotions—how easily any of these lead to prayer which has no spiritual power and avails but little. For true prayer—that takes hold of God's strength, that avails much, to which the gates of heaven are really opened wide—who would not cry, "Oh, for someone to teach me to pray in that way!"

Jesus has opened a school for training His redeemed ones who specially desire to have power in prayer. Shall we not enter it with the petition, "Lord, it is just this we need to be taught! Oh, teach us to *pray*!"

We have read in your Word with what power your believing people of old used to pray and what mighty wonders were done in answer to their prayers. If this took place under the Old Covenant, in the time of preparation, how much more in these days of fulfillment will you give your people this sure sign of your presence in their midst. We have heard the promises given to your apostles about the power of prayer in your name. We have seen how gloriously they experienced the truth of those promises. We know for certain they can become true to us too. Even in these days we hear continually what glorious tokens of your power you still give to those who trust you fully. Lord, all of these are men of like passions with ourselves; teach *us* to pray that way too. The promises are for us. The powers and gifts of the heavenly world are for us. Teach *us* to pray so that we may receive abundantly. To us too you have entrusted your work. On our prayer, too the coming of your kingdom depends. In prayer too you can glorify your name. Yes, *us*, Lord, we offer ourselves as learners. We would indeed be taught of Thee.

We feel the need now of being *taught* to pray. At first there is no work which appears so simple. Later on, none that is more difficult. Then the confession is forced from us that we know not to pray as we ought. It is true we have God's Word, with its clear and sure promises, but sin has so darkened our mind that we do not always know how to apply the Word. In spiritual things we do not always seek the most needful things, or we fail in praying according to the law of the sanctuary. In temporal things we are still less able to avail ourselves of the wonderful liberty our Father has given us to ask what we need. Even when we know what to ask, how much is still needed to make prayer acceptable. It must be to the glory of God, in full surrender to His will, in full assurance of faith, in the name of Jesus, and with a perseverance that refuses to be denied. All this must be learned. It can be learned only in the school of much prayer, for it is practice which perfects. Amid the painful consciousness of ignorance and unworthiness and in the struggle between believing and doubting, the heavenly art of effective prayer is learned. Because, even when we do not remember it, there is One—the beginner and finisher of faith and prayer—who watches over our praying and sees to it that *in all who trust Him for it* their education in the school of prayer shall be carried on to perfection. Let the deep undertone of all our prayer be the teachableness that comes from a sense of ignorance and from faith in Him as a perfect teacher. Then we shall be taught. We shall learn to pray in power. We may depend upon it, He *teaches* to pray.

A pupil needs a teacher who knows his work and has the gift of teaching, who in patience and love will descend to the pupil's needs. Jesus is all this and much more. No one can teach like

16

Jesus. It is Jesus, praying himself, who teaches to pray. He knows what prayer is. He learned it in the trials and tears of His earthly life. In heaven it is still His beloved work; His life there is prayer. Nothing delights Him more than to find those whom He can take with Him into the Father's presence. He can clothe them with power to pray down God's blessing on those around them. He can train to be His fellow workers in the intercession by which the kingdom is to be revealed on earth. He knows how to teach. Now by the urgency of felt need, then by the confidence with which joy inspires. Here by the teaching of the Word, there by the testimony of another believer who knows what it is to have prayer heard. By His Holy Spirit, He has access to our heart and shows us the sin that hinders prayer or gives us the assurance that we please God. He teaches not only by thoughts of what to ask or how to ask, but by breathing within us the very spirit of prayer, by living within us as the Great Intercessor. In awe and joy we ask, "Who teaches like him?"

Jesus taught His disciples not how to preach, only how to pray. He spoke little of what was needed to preach well but much of praying well. To know how to speak to God is more vital than knowing how to speak to man. Not power with men but power with God is of supreme importance. Jesus loves to teach us how to pray.

As we meditate on the words He spoke on earth, let us yield ourselves to His teaching on the art of prayer in the fullest confidence that, with such a teacher, we shall make progress. Let us not only meditate but pray and wait at the foot of the throne to be trained for the work of intercession—in assurance that even in our stammerings and fears He is carrying on His work most beautifully. He will breathe into us His own life, which is all prayer. As He makes us partakers of His righteousness and His life, He will of His intercession too. As the members of His body, as a holy priesthood, we shall take part in His priestly work of pleading and prevailing with God for men. Ignorant and feeble as we are, Lord, teach us to pray.

Blessed Lord, you ever live to pray and you can teach me, too, to pray and to ever live to pray. You love to make me share your glory in heaven by my praying without ceasing and by my standing as a priest in the presence of my God.

Lord Jesus, I confess I know not how to pray as I ought. Teach me to tarry with you and so give you time to train me to pray. May a deep sense of my ignorance, of the wonderful privilege and power of prayer and of the need of the Holy Spirit as the Spirit of prayer, lead me to cast away my thoughts of what I think I know. Make me kneel before you in true teachableness and poverty of spirit.

Fill me, Lord, with confidence that with a teacher like you, I shall learn to pray. With Jesus as my teacher—He who ever prays to the Father and by His prayer rules the destinies of His Church and the world—I will not be afraid. As much as I need to know of the mysteries of the prayer-world, you will unfold for me. And when I may not know, you will teach me to be strong in faith, giving glory to God.

Blessed Lord, you will not put to shame your scholar who trusts you, nor, by your grace, would he put you to shame either. Amen.

LESSON TWO

The Worshippers

"But the hour cometh, and now is, when the true worshippers shall worship the Father in spirit and in truth: for the Father seeketh such to worship him. God is a spirit: and they that worship him must worship him in spirit and in truth" (John 4:23, 24).

Jesus' words to the woman of Samaria are His first recorded teaching on prayer. They give us some wonderful first glimpses into the world of prayer. The Father *seeks* worshippers. Our worship satisfies His loving heart and is a joy to Him. He seeks *true worshippers* but does not find many. True worship is that which is *in spirit and truth. The Son has come* to open the way for this worship in spirit and truth and teach it to us. One of our first lessons in the school of prayer must be to understand what it means to pray in spirit and in truth and to know how we can do so.

To the woman of Samaria our Lord spoke of a threefold worship. There is first, the ignorant worship of the Samaritans: "Ye worship ye know not what." The second, the intelligent worship of the Jew, having the true knowledge of God: "we know what we worship: for salvation is of the Jews." And then the new, the spiritual worship which He himself has come to introduce: "But the hour cometh, and now is, when the true worshippers shall

18

worship the Father in spirit and in truth." From the connection it is evident that the words "in spirit and in truth" do not mean, as is often thought, earnestly, from the heart, in sincerity. The Samaritans had the five books of Moses and some knowledge of God; there was doubtless more than one among them who honestly and earnestly sought God in prayer. The Jews had the true full revelation of God in His word as thus far given; there were among them godly men who called upon God with their whole heart. But still not "in spirit and in truth" in the full meaning of the words. Jesus says, *The hour cometh, and now is*"; it is only in and through Him that the worship of God will be in spirit and in truth.

Among Christians one still finds the three classes of worshippers. Some who in their ignorance hardly know what they ask. They pray earnestly, and yet receive but little. Others with more knowledge, try to pray with all their mind and heart—often most earnestly but do not attain the full blessedness of worship in spirit and truth. We must ask our Lord Jesus to take us into this third class; we must be taught of Him how to worship in spirit and truth. This alone is spiritual worship. This makes us worshippers such as the Father seeks. In prayer everything will depend on our understanding well and practicing the worship in spirit and truth.

"God is a *Spirit*, and they that worship him must worship him *in spirit* and in truth." The first thought suggested here by the Master is that there must be harmony between God and His worshippers; such as God is, so must His worship be. This obeys a principle which prevails throughout the universe: we look for correspondence between an object and the organ to which it reveals or yields itself. The eye has an inner fitness for the light, the ear for sound. The man who would truly worship God, who would find, know, possess, and enjoy God must be in harmony with Him and have the capacity for receiving Him. Because God *is Spirit*, we must worship *in spirit*. As God is, so His worshipper must be.

What does this mean? The woman asked our Lord whether Samaria or Jerusalem was the true place of worship. He answers that from this time on worship is no longer to be limited to a certain place: "Woman, believe me, *the hour cometh,* when ye shall neither in this mountain, nor yet at Jerusalem, worship the Father." As God is Spirit—not bound by space or time but in His infinite perfection always and everywhere the same—so His worship now is no longer to be confined by place or form, but spiritual as God himself is spiritual. That is a lesson of deep importance. How much our Christianity suffers because it is confined to certain times and places. A man who seeks to pray earnestly in the church or in the closet spends the greater part of the week or the day in a spirit entirely at variance from that in which he prayed. His worship was the work of a fixed place or hour and not of his whole being. God is a Spirit. He is the everlasting and unchangeable one. What He is, He is always and in truth. Our worship must also be in spirit and truth. His worship must be the spirit of our life. Our life must be worship in spirit as God is Spirit.

The second thought that comes to us is that this worship in the spirit must come from God himself. God is Spirit. He alone has Spirit to give. It was for this He sent His Son to fit us for such spiritual worship by giving us the Holy Spirit. It is of His own work that Jesus speaks when He says twice, "The hour cometh," and then adds, "and now is." He came to baptize with the Holy Spirit; the Spirit could not stream forth until He was glorified (John 1:33; 7:37, 38; 16:7). It was when He had made an end of sin, and entering into the Holiest of all with His blood, had there on our behalf *received* the Holy Spirit (Acts 2:33), that He could send Him down to us as the Spirit of the Father. It was when Christ had redeemed us, and we in Him had received the position of children, that the Father sent forth the Spirit of His Son into our hearts to cry, "Abba, Father." The worship in spirit means the worship of the Father in the Spirit of Christ, the Spirit of Sonship.

This is the reason why Jesus here uses the name of Father. We never find one of the Old Testament saints who personally appropriates the name of child or calls God his Father. The worship *of the Father* is only possible to those to whom the Spirit of the Son has been given. The worship *in spirit* is only possible to those to whom the Son has revealed the Father, and who have received the spirit of Sonship. It is only Christ who opens the way and teaches the worship in spirit.

In truth does not only mean *in sincerity*. Nor does it only signify in accordance with the truth of God's Word. The expression is one of deep and divine meaning. Jesus is "the only-begotten of the Father, *full of* grace and *truth*." "The law was given by Moses; grace and *truth came* by Jesus Christ." Jesus says, "*I am the truth* and the life." In the Old Testament all was shadow and promise. Jesus brought and gives the reality, *the substance*, of things hoped for. In Him the blessings and powers of the eternal life are our actual possession and experience. Jesus is full of grace and truth. The Holy Spirit is the Spirit of truth. Through Him the grace that is in Jesus is ours in deed and truth, a positive communication out of the divine life. So worship in spirit is worship *in truth*, actual living fellowship with God, with a real correspondence and harmony between the Father, who is a Spirit, and the child praying in the spirit.

What Jesus said to the woman of Samaria, she could not at once understand. Pentecost was needed to reveal its full meaning. We are hardly prepared at our first entrance into the school of prayer to grasp such teaching. We shall understand it better later on. Let us only begin and take the lesson as He gives it. We are carnal and cannot bring God the worship He seeks. But Jesus came to give the Spirit. He has given Him to us. Let the disposition in which we set ourselves to pray be what Christ's words have taught us. Let there be the deep confession of our inability to bring God the worship that is pleasing to Him, the childlike teachableness that waits on Him to instruct us, and the simple faith that yields itself to the breathing of the Spirit. Above all, let us hold fast the blessed truth that the knowledge of the Fatherhood of God, the revelation of His infinite Fatherliness in our hearts, the faith in the infinite love that gives us His Son and His Spirit to make us children is indeed the secret of prayer in spirit and truth. This is the new and living way Christ opened up for us. To have Christ the Son and *the Spirit of the Son* dwelling within us and revealing the Father, this makes us true, spiritual worshippers.

Blessed Lord, I adore the love with which you did teach a woman, who had refused you a cup of water, what the worship of God must be. I rejoice in the assurance that you will no less now instruct your disciple, who comes to you with a heart that longs to pray in spirit and in truth. O my Holy Master, do teach me this blessed secret.

Teach me that the worship in spirit and truth is not of man but only comes from you; that it is not only a thing of times and seasons, but the outflowing of a life in you. Teach me to draw near to God in prayer with a deep awareness of my ignorance and my having nothing in myself to offer Him, and at the same time of the provision that you, my Saviour, make for the Spirit's breathing in my childlike stammerings. I do bless you that in you I am a child and have a child's liberty of access, that in you I have the spirit of Sonship and of worship in truth. Teach me, above all, blessed Son of the Father, how it is the revelation of the Father that gives confidence in prayer. Let the infinite Fatherliness of God's heart be my joy and strength for a life of prayer and of worship. Amen.

Alone with God

"But thou, when thou prayest, enter into thy closet, and when thou hast shut thy door, pray to thy Father which is in secret; and thy Father which seeth in secret shall reward thee openly" (Matt. 6:6).

Jesus gave His first disciples their first public teaching in the Sermon on the Mount. He expounded to them the kingdom of God, its laws and its life. In that kingdom God is not only King, but Father. He not only gives all but is himself all. In the knowledge and fellowship of Him alone is its blessedness. So the revelation of prayer and the prayer life was a part of His teaching concerning the new kingdom He came to set up. Moses gave neither command nor regulation with regard to prayer. Even the prophets say little directly about the duty of prayer. It is Christ who teaches to pray.

The first thing the Lord teaches His disciples is that they must have a secret place for prayer. Everyone must have some solitary spot where he can be alone with his God. Every teacher must have a schoolroom. Jesus is our only teacher in the school of prayer. He already taught us at Samaria that worship is no longer confined to times and places; but that true spiritual worship is a thing of the spirit and the life. The whole man must in his whole life be worship in spirit and truth. He wants each one to choose for himself the fixed spot where Jesus can daily meet him. That inner room, that solitary place, is Jesus' schoolroom. That spot may be anywhere. That spot may change from day to day if we have to change our abode, but there must be a secret place and a quiet time in which the pupil places himself in the Master's presence, to be prepared by Him to worship the Father. There Jesus comes to us to teach us to pray.

A teacher wants his schoolroom to be bright and attractive, light and airy, a place where pupils want to come and love to stay. In the Sermon on the Mount, Jesus seeks to set the place of prayer before us in its most attractive light. We soon notice what is the most important thing He has to tell us about our waiting there. Three times He uses the name of Father: "Pray to *thy Father*," "*Thy Father* shall recompense thee," "*Your Father* knoweth what things ye have need of." The first need in closet-prayer is: "I must meet my Father." The light that shines in the closet must be the light of the Father's countenance. The fresh air from heaven with which Jesus would have it filled—the atmosphere in which I am to breathe and pray—is God's Father-love, God's infinite fatherliness. Thus each thought or petition we breathe out will be simple, hearty, childlike trust in the Father. This is how the Master teaches us to pray. He brings us into the Father's living presence. What we pray there must accomplish much.

"Pray to thy Father which is in secret." God hides himself to the carnal eye. In worship as long as we are primarily occupied with our own thoughts and exercises, we shall not meet Him who is a Spirit, the unseen One. But to the man who withdraws himself from all that is of the world and man and prepares to wait upon God alone, the Father will reveal himself. As he forsakes and shuts out the life of the world and surrenders himself to be led of Christ into the secret of God's presence, the light of the Father's love will rise upon him. The secrecy of the inner room and the closed door, the entire separation from all around us, is an image of that inner spiritual sanctuary, the secret of God's tabernacle within the veil, where our spirit truly comes into

contact with the invisible One. So at the very outset of our search
after the secret of effective prayer, we are taught that it is in the
inner room alone with the Father that we shall learn to pray
aright. In the words "The Father which is in secret," Jesus teaches us where He is waiting for us, where He is always to be found.

Christians often complain that private prayer is not what it
should be. They feel weak and sinful. The heart is cold and dark.
It is as if they have so little to pray, and in that little no faith or
joy. They are discouraged and kept from prayer by the thought
that they cannot come to the Father as they ought to or as they
wish. Your Teacher tells you that when you go to private prayer,
your first thought must be, "The Father is in secret; He waits for
me there." Just because your heart is cold and prayerless, go into
the presence of the loving Father. As a father pities his children,
so the Lord pities you. Do not think of how little you have to
bring God, but of how much He wants to give you. Look up into
His face. Think of His wonderful, tender, pitying love. Tell Him
how sinful and cold and dark all is. The Father's loving heart will
give light and warmth to yours. Do what Jesus says. Shut the
door and pray to thy Father which is in secret. Is it not wonderful
to be able to be alone with the infinite God? Look up and say,
"My Father!"

"And thy Father which seeth in secret will recompense thee."
Jesus assures us that secret prayer cannot be fruitless. Its blessing will be shown in our life. In secret, alone with God, if we entrust our life before men to Him, then He will reward us openly.
He will see to it that the answer to prayer be made manifest in
His blessing upon us. Our Lord would teach us that just as God
meets us in secret with infinite fatherliness and faithfulness, so
we should have the childlike simplicity of faith and confidence
that our prayer does bring down a blessing.

"He that cometh to God must believe that He is rewarder of
them that seek him." The blessing of the closet does not depend
on the strong or fervent feeling with which I pray, but upon the
love and the power of the Father to whom I there entrust my
needs. Therefore the Master has but one desire: Remember your
Father is, and sees, and hears in secret. Go there and stay there,
and then go out from there in confidence that He will recom-

pense. Trust Him for it. Depend upon Him. Prayer to the Father cannot be vain. He will reward you openly.

To confirm this faith in the Father-love of God, Christ speaks a third word: *"Your Father knoweth what things ye have need of before ye ask him."* At first sight it might appear as if this thought made prayer less needful. God knows far better than we what we need. But as we get a deeper insight into what prayer really is, this truth will help much to strengthen our faith. It will teach us that we do not need, as the heathen do, to use many and urgent pleas to compel an unwilling God to listen to us. It will lead to a holy thoughtfulness and silence in prayer as we ask, "Does my Father really know that I need this?" When once the Spirit gives certainity that our request, according to the Word, is needed for God's glory, we can say with wonderful confidence, "My Father knows I need it and must have it." If there be any delay in the answer, it will teach us in quiet perseverance to hold on. *Father! You know* I need it. Christ, our teacher, wants to cultivate the blessed liberty and simplicity of a child in us as we draw near to God. Let us look up to the Father until His Spirit works it in us. In our prayers, when we are sometimes in danger of being so occupied with fervent, urgent petitions, as to forget that the Father knows and hears, let us hold still and just quietly say, "My Father sees, He hears, He knows." It will help our faith to claim the answer, and to say, "We know that we have the petitions we have asked of him."

Now take these lessons, practice them, and trust Him to perfect you in them. Dwell much in the inner toom, with the door shut—shut away from men, shut up with God. There the Father waits for you. There Jesus will teach you to pray. To be alone in secret with the Father: may this be your highest joy. To be assured that the Father will openly reward the secret prayer, so that it cannot remain unblessed—may this be your strength day by day. To know that the Father knows that you need what you ask will give you liberty to bring every need, in the assurance that your God will supply it according to His riches in glory in Christ Jesus.

Blessed Saviour, with my whole heart I bless you for the

appointment of the inner room as the school where you meet each of your pupils alone, and reveal to him the Father. My Lord, strengthen my faith in the Father's tender love and kindness, so that my first instinctive thought, when sinful or troubled, may be to go where I know the Father awaits me and where prayer never can go unblessed. Let the thought that He knows my need before I ask bring me in great restfulness of faith, to trust that He will give what His child requires. Let the place of secret prayer become to me the most beloved spot of earth.

Lord, hear me as I pray that you would everywhere bless the closets of your believing people. Let your wonderful revelation of a Father's tenderness free all young Christians from every thought of secret prayer as a duty or a burden and lead them to regard it as the highest privilege of their life, a joy and a blessing. Bring back all who are discouraged because they cannot find anything to bring to you in prayer. May they see they only need to come with their emptiness to Him who has all to give—and delights to do it. Let their one thought be not what they have to bring the Father, but what the Father waits to give them.

Bless especially the inner room of all your servants as the place where God's truth and grace are revealed to them, where they are daily anointed with fresh oil, where their strength is renewed, and the blessings with which they are to bless their fellowmen are received in faith. Lord, draw us all in the closet nearer to yourself and the Father. Amen.

LESSON FOUR

The Model Prayer

"After this manner therefore pray ye: Our Father which art in heaven" (Matt. 6:9).

Every teacher knows the power of example. He not only tells the child what to do and how to do it, but shows him how it really can be done. In condescension to our weakness, our heavenly teacher has given us the very words we are to use as we draw near to our Father. We have in them a form of prayer in which there breathes the freshness and fullness of the eternal life. So simple that the child can lisp it, so divinely rich that it takes in all that God can give. A form of prayer that becomes the model and inspiration for all other prayer and yet always draws us back to itself as the deepest utterance of our souls before our God.

"Our Father which art in heaven!" To appreciate this word of adoration fully, remember that none of the saints had in Scripture ever ventured to address God as their Father. The invocation places us at once in the center of the wonderful revelation the Son came to make of His Father being our Father too. It encompasses the mystery of redemption—Christ delivering us from the curse that we might become the children of God. The mystery of regeneration—the Spirit in the new birth giving us the

28

new life. And the mystery of faith—even before the redemption is accomplished or understood, the word is given to the disciples to prepare them for the blessed experience still to come.

The words are the key to the whole prayer, to all prayer. It takes time to study them. It will take eternity to understand them fully. The knowledge of God's Father-love is the first and simplest—but also the last and highest—lesson in the school of prayer. It is in the personal relation to the living God, and the personal conscious fellowship of love with Him, that prayer begins. It is in the knowledge of God's fatherliness revealed by the Holy Spirit that the power of prayer will take root and grow. In the infinite tenderness and pity and patience of the infinite Father, in His loving readiness to hear and to help, the life of prayer has its joy. Let us take time for the Spirit to make these words spirit and truth to us, filling heart and life: "Our Father which are in heaven." Then we are indeed within the veil, in the secret place of power where prayer always prevails.

"Hallowed be thy name." While we ordinarily first bring our own needs to God in prayer, and then think of what belongs to God and His interests, the Master reverses the order. First, *Thy* name, *Thy* kingdom, *Thy* will; then, give *us*, forgive *us*, lead *us*, deliver *us*. The lesson is more important than we think. In true worship the Father must be first, must be all. The sooner I learn to forget myself in the desire that He may be glorified, the richer will the blessing be that prayer will bring to me. No one ever loses by what he sacrifices for the Father.

This must influence all our prayer. There are two types of prayer: personal and intercessory. The latter ordinarily occupies the lesser part of our time and energy. But Christ has opened the school of prayer especially to train intercessors for the great work of bringing down, by their faith and prayer, the blessings of His work and love upon the world around. Unless this is our aim there can be no deep growth in prayer. A little child may ask of the father only what he needs for himself, although he soon learns to ask, "Give some for my sister, too." But the grown-up son who only lives for the father's interest and to care for his father's business, asks for bigger things and gets all that is asked.

Jesus wants to train us to the blessed life of consecration and service in which our interests are all subordinate to the name, the kingdom, and the will of the Father. So let each act of adoration to "Our Father!" be followed in the same breath by "*Thy* name, *Thy* kingdom, *Thy* will."

"*Hallowed be thy name.*" What name? This new name of Father. The word *holy* is the central word of the Old Testament, the name *Father of* the New. All the holiness and glory of God are now to be revealed in this name of love. But how is the name to be hallowed? By God himself. "*I will hallow* my great name which ye have profaned." Our prayer must be that in all and everywhere God himself would reveal the holiness and divine power, the hidden glory of the name of Father. The Spirit of the Father is the *Holy Spirit*. Only when we yield ourselves to be led *of Him*, will the name be *hallowed* in our prayers and our lives.

"*Thy kingdom come.*" The Father is a King and has a kingdom. The son and heir of a king has no higher ambition than the glory of his father's kingdom. In time of war or danger this becomes his passion. He can think of nothing else. The children of the Father are here in the enemy's territory where the kingdom—which is in heaven—is not yet fully manifested. When they learn to hallow the Father-name, what is more natural than that they should long and cry with deep enthusiasm, "Thy kingdom come"? The coming of the kingdom is the one great event on which the revelation of the Father's glory, the blessedness of His children, and the salvation of the world depends. The coming of the kingdom waits on our prayers. Shall we not join in the deep longing cry of the redeemed, "Thy kingdom come"? Let us learn it in the school of Jesus.

"*Thy will be done in earth, as it is in heaven.*" Too frequently this petition is applied only to the *suffering* of the will of God. In heaven God's will is *done* and the Master teaches the child to ask that the will may be done on earth just as in heaven—in the spirit of adoring submission and ready obedience. Because the will of God is the glory of heaven, the doing of it is the blessedness of heaven. As the will is done, the kingdom of heaven comes into the heart. Wherever faith has accepted the Father's love, obedience accepts the Father's will. Surrender to and prayer for a life of heaven-like obedience is the spirit of childlike prayer.

"Give us this day our daily bread." When the child has first yielded himself to the Father in concern for His name, His kingdom, and His will, he has full liberty to ask for his own daily bread. A master cares for the food of his servant, a general of his soldiers, a father of his child. Will not the Father in heaven care for the child who has in prayer given himself up to His interests? In full confidence we may say, "Father, I live for your honor and your work. I know you care for me." Consecration to God and His will gives wonderful liberty in prayer for temporal things because the whole earthly life is given over to the Father's loving care.

"And forgive us our debts, as we forgive our debtors." As bread is the first need of the body, so forgiveness is for the soul. The provision for the one is as sure as for the others. We are children but we are also sinners. Our right of access to the Father's presence we owe to the precious blood and the forgiveness it has won for us. Let us beware of the prayer for forgiveness becoming a formality. Only what is really confessed is really forgiven. Let us in faith accept the forgiveness as promised as a spiritual reality and an actual transaction between God and us. It is the entrance into all the privileges of children. Such forgiveness as a living experience is impossible without a forgiving spirit to others; because just as *forgiven* expresses the heavenward so *forgiving* expresses the earthward relation of God's child. When I pray, I must be able to say that I know of no one whom I do not heartily love.

"And lead us not into temptation, but deliver us from the evil one." In these three petitions—our daily bread, the pardon of our sins, our being kept from all sin and the power of the evil one—all our personal need is included. The prayer for bread and pardon must be accompanied by the total surrender to live in holy obedience to the Father's will and by believing prayer to be kept in everything from the power of the evil one by the power of the indwelling Spirit.

Jesus wants us to pray this way to the Father in heaven. Let His name, and kingdom, and will have first place in our love; then His providing, pardoning and keeping love will be our sure portion. So the prayer will guide us to the true child-life—the

Father being all to the child, the Father being all for the child.
We shall understand how Father and child, the *Your* and the *our*,
are all one, and how the heart that begins its prayer with the
God-devoted *your* will have the power in faith to speak out the
our too. Such prayer will be the fellowship and interchange of
love, always bringing us back in trust and worship to Him who is
not only the Beginning but the End. "For thine is the kingdom,
and the power, and the glory, forever, Amen."

*You who are the only-begotten Son, teach us to pray, "Our
Father." Thank you, Lord, for these living blessed words which
you have given to us. We thank you for the millions who in them
have learned to know and worship the Father. Thank you for
what they have been to us. Lord, it seems we need days and
weeks in your school with each separate petition—so deep and
full are they. But we look to you to lead us deeper into their
meaning. Do it, we pray, for your name's sake; your name is Son
of the Father.*

*Lord, you once said, "No man knoweth the Father save the
Son, and he to whom the Son willeth to reveal him." And again,
"I made known unto them thy name, and will make it known,
that the love wherewith thou hast loved me may be in them."
Lord Jesus, reveal the Father to us. Let His name, His infinite
Father-love, the love with which He loved you, according to your
prayer, be in us. Then shall we say truthfully, "Our Father!"
Then we will obey your teaching, and the first spontaneous
breathing of our heart will be, "Our Father, your name, your
kingdom, your will." Our needs and our sins and our temptations
we will bring to Him in the confidence that the love of such a
Father cares for all.*

*Blessed Lord, we are your students. We trust you. Do teach us
to pray, "Our Father." Amen.*

LESSON FIVE

The Certainty of the Answer to Prayer

"Ask and it *shall* be given you; seek, and ye *shall* find; knock, and it *shall* be opened unto you: for every one that asketh *receiveth*; and he that seeketh *findeth*; and to him that knocketh it *shall be opened*" (Matt. 7:7, 8).

"Ye ask, and *receive not,* because ye ask amiss" (Jas. 4:3).

Our Lord returns here to speak of prayer again in the Sermon on the Mount. The first time he told about the Father who is to be found in secret and rewards openly, and gave us the pattern prayer (Matt. 6:5-15). Here He wants to teach us what all Scripture considers the most important thing in prayer: that prayer will be heard and answered. He uses words which mean almost the same thing, and each time He repeats the promise so distinctly: "Ye *shall* receive, ye *shall* find, it *shall* be opened unto you." Then he gives the law of the kingdom as the basis for such assurance. "He that asketh, *receiveth;* he that seeketh, *findeth;* to him that knocketh, *it shall be opened.*" In all this repetition, we can see that He wants to implant in our minds the truth that we may—and must—confidently expect an answer to our prayer. Next to the revelation of the Father's love, there is no more important lesson in the whole school of prayer than this: Everyone that asks receives.

33

A difference of meaning has been sought in the three words: *ask, seek, knock*. The first, ask, refers to the gifts we pray for. But I may ask for and receive a gift without the Giver. Seek is the word Scripture uses of God himself. Christ assures me that I can find God. But it is not enough to find God in time of need without also coming into an abiding fellowship. Knock speaks of being admitted to dwell with Him and in Him. Asking and receiving the gift thus leads to seeking and finding the Giver. This again leads to the knocking and opening of the door to the Father's home and love. One thing is sure: the Lord does want us to believe with certainty that asking, seeking and knocking cannot be in vain. Receiving an answer, finding God, the opened heart and home of God, are the certain fruit of prayer.

It is significant that the Lord should have thought it necessary to repeat the truth in so many forms. It proves that He knows our heart, how doubt and distrust toward God are natural to us, and how easily we are inclined to rest in prayer as a religious duty without expecting an answer. He knows too how, even when we believe that God is the hearer of prayer, we still may feel that believing prayer that claims God's promise to answer is something spiritual, too high and difficult for the half-hearted disciple. So at the very outset of His instruction on prayer, He seeks to lodge this truth deep into their hearts: prayer does accomplish much. Ask and ye *shall* receive; *every one* that asks receives. This is the fixed eternal law of the kingdom. So if you ask and do not receive, it must be because there is something wrong or lacking in the prayer.

Persevere; let the Word and the Spirit teach you to pray in the right way and do not let go of the confidence He seeks to arouse that everyone who asks receives an answer.

Christ has no mightier stimulus to persevering prayer in His school than this. As a child has to prove a mathematical sum correct, so the proof that we have prayed correctly is *our answer*. If we ask and receive not, it is because we have not learned to pray in the right way. Let every learner in the school of Christ therefore believe the Master's promises to answer in all simplicity. He had good reasons for speaking so unconditionally. Let us beware of weakening the Word with our human wisdom. When He tells us heavenly things, let us believe Him. His Word will explain itself to him who believes it fully. If questions and difficulties arise, let us not seek to have them settled before we accept the Word. No, let us entrust them all to Him. It is His work to solve them. Our work is first and fully to accept and hold fast His promise.

According to the Master's teaching, prayer has two sides, a human and a divine. The human is the asking, the divine is the giving. Or to look at both from the human side, there is the asking and the receiving—the two halves that make up a whole. He tells us that we are not to rest without an answer because it is the will of God—the rule in the Father's family—that every childlike believing petition is granted. If no answer comes, we are not to sit down in the sloth that calls itself resignation and suppose that it is not God's will to give an answer. No. Something in the prayer must not be as God would have it—childlike and believing. We must seek for grace to pray so that the answer may come. It is far easier to the flesh to submit without the answer than to yield itself to be searched and purified by the Spirit, until it has learned to pray the prayer of faith.

One of the terrible marks of the diseased state of Christian life in these days is that there are so many who rest content without specific answers to prayer. They pray daily, they ask many things, and trust that some of them will be heard, but know little of direct definite answer to prayer as the rule of daily life. But it is this the Father wills. He seeks a daily interaction with His children in listening to and granting their petitions. He wills that I should come to Him day by day with distinct requests; He wills day by day to do for me what I ask. In His answers to prayer the saints of old learned to know God as the Living One, and were stirred to praise and love (Ps. 34; 66; 19; 116:1). Our Teacher waits to imprint upon our minds that prayer and its answer, the child asking and the father giving, are inseparably linked.

Sometimes the answer is a refusal, because the request is not according to God's Word, just as when Moses asked to enter Canaan. But there was an answer. God did not leave His servant in uncertainty as to His will. The gods of the heathen are dumb and cannot speak. Our Father lets His child know when He cannot give him what he asks. Then the child can withdraw his petition, just as the Son did in Gethsemane. Both Moses the servant and Christ the Son knew that what they asked was not according to what the Lord had spoken; their prayer was the humble supplication whether it was possible for the decision to be changed. By His Word and Spirit, God will teach those who are teachable; give Him time and He will show them whether or not their request is according to His will. Let us withdraw the request if it is not according to God's mind. If it is, let us persevere till the answer comes. Prayer is appointed to us to obtain an answer. In prayer and its answer the interchange of love between the Father and His child takes place.

How deep the estrangement of our heart from God must be, that we find it so difficult to grasp such promises. Although we may accept the words and believe their truth, the faith of the heart that fully trusts and rejoices in them comes so slowly. Because our spiritual life is still so weak and our capacity for thinking God's thoughts is so feeble, let us look to Jesus to teach us as none but He can. If we take His words in simplicity, and trust Him by His Spirit to make them within us life and power, they will so enter into our inner being that the divine spiritual reality of their truth will indeed possess us, and we shall not rest content until every petition we offer is sent heavenward on Jesus' own words: "Ask, and it shall be given you."

Let us set ourselves to learn this lesson well and take these words just as they were spoken. Do not let human reason weaken their force. Simply take them as Jesus gives them, and believe them. In due time He will teach us to understand them fully. Let us begin by implicitly believing them. Do not allow the feeble experiences of our unbelief to be the measure of what our faith may expect. At all times let us believe in joyful assurance that man's prayer on earth and God's answer in heaven are meant for each other. Trust Jesus to teach us to pray, so that the answer can come. He will do it if we hold fast His words: "Ask, and ye shall receive."

Lord Jesus, teach me to understand and believe what you promise me. You know how my heart seeks to satisfy itself, when no answer comes. Is my prayer in harmony with the Father's secret counsel? Is there something better you would give me? Is prayer as fellowship with you blessing enough without expecting an answer? But, Lord I find in your teaching on prayer that you did not say these things, but said plainly that prayer MAY and MUST expect an answer. You assured us that the child asks and the Father gives.

Lord, your words are faithful and true. I do not receive, so I must be praying in the wrong way. It must be—because I live too little in the Spirit—that my prayer is too little of the Spirit, and that the power for the prayer of faith is lacking.

Lord Jesus, teach me to pray in faith and remember that everyone that asks receives. Amen.

The Infinite Fatherliness of God

"Or what man is there of you, whom if his son ask bread, will he give him a stone? Or if he ask a fish, will he give him a serpent? If ye then, being evil, know how to give good gifts unto your children, how much more shall your Father which is in heaven give good things to them that ask him?" (Matt. 7:9-11).

Our Lord confirms further what He had said of the certainty of an answer to prayer. To remove all doubt and show us on what sure ground His promise rests, He appeals to a truth all have seen and experienced here on earth. We are all children, and know what we expected of our fathers. Everywhere we look upon it as a most natural thing for a father to hear his child. And the Lord asks us to look up from earthly parents—of whom the best are but evil—and to calculate *how much more* the heavenly Father will give good gifts to them that ask Him. Jesus shows us that, as much greater as God is than sinful man, *so much greater* our assurance should be that God will grant our childlike petitions—more surely than any earthly father. As much greater as God is than man, *so much surer* is it that prayer will be heard with the Father in heaven than with a father on earth.

This parable is simple and intelligible. Equally deep and spiritual is the teaching it contains. The Lord reminds us that the prayer of a child is influenced entirely by the relation which he has with the parent. Prayer can exert that influence only when the child is really living and walking in a loving relationship in the home and in the service of the Father. The power of the promise, "Ask, and it shall be given you," lies in that good relationship. Then the prayer of faith and its answer will be the natural result. Today the lesson is: Live as a child of God and then you may pray as a child with complete certainty of an answer.

What is the mark of a true child? The child who by choice forsakes the father's house and finds no pleasure in the presence and love and obedience of the father—who still expects to ask and obtain what he will—will surely be disappointed. On the contrary, he to whom the love and will of the father are the joy of his life will find that it is the father's joy to grant his requests. Scripture says, "As many as are *led* by the Spirit of God, they are the children of God." The childlike privilege of asking all is inseparable from the childlike life under the leading of the Spirit. He who yields himself to be led by the Spirit in his life will be led by Him in his prayers too. He will find that fatherlike giving is the divine response to childlike living.

What is this childlike living on which childlike asking and believing are grounded? In the Sermon on the Mount our Lord teaches about the Father and His children. In it the prayer-promises He gives are inseparably imbedded in the life-precepts. They form one whole. He alone can count on the fulfillment of the promise, who also accepts all that the Lord links with it.

In saying, "Ask, and ye shall receive," He implies: I give these promises to those whom in the Beatitudes I have pictured in their childlike poverty and purity, and of whom I have said, 'They shall be called the children of God' (Matt. 5:3-9); to children, who 'let your light shine before men, so that they may glorify your Father in heaven'; to those who walk in love, 'that ye may be children of your Father which is in heaven,' and who seek to be perfect 'even as your Father in heaven is perfect' (5:45); to those whose fasting and praying and almsgiving (6:1-18) is not before men, but 'before your Father which seeth in secret'; who forgive 'even as your Father forgiveth you' (6:15); who trust the heavenly Father for all earthly need, seeking first the kingdom of

God and His righteousness (6:26-32); who not only say, Lord, Lord, but do the will of my Father which is in heaven (7:21). Such are the children of the Father and such is the life in the Father's love and service. In such a childlife answered prayers are certain and abundant.

Is this teaching discouraging? Can we hope for answers to prayer if we must first be children like that? Yes, we can if we remember the comforting comparison of father and child. A child is weak; children differ much in age and talents. But the Lord demands not a perfect fulfillment of the law, but only a childlike, wholehearted surrender to Him in obedience and truth. Nothing more—and nothing less. The Father asks the whole heart. Then when He sees the child honestly, consistently seeking to live as a child, then He will consider the prayer as the prayer of a child. If anyone simply and honestly begins to study the Sermon on the Mount and takes it as his guide, he will find—in spite of weakness and failure—an ever-increasing liberty to claim fulfillment of promises about prayer. In "father" and "child" he has the pledge that his petitions will be granted.

This is Jesus' main thought here. He wants us to know the secret of effective prayer: a heart filled with the Father-love of God. It is not enough for us to know that God is a Father. He wants us to understand fully all that name implies. Take the best earthly father we know. Think of the tenderness and love he gives to the request of his child, and the joy with which he grants every reasonable desire. Then think in adoring worship of the infinite love and fatherliness of God and consider with *how much more* tenderness and joy *He* sees us come and gives us what we ask.

Is this beyond our understanding? Is it impossible for us to believe God's readiness to hear us? Then let the Holy Spirit shed abroad God's Father-love in our heart not only when we pray, but with a yielded heart and life that dwell always in that love. The child who only wants to know the love of the father when he has something to ask will be disappointed. But he who lets God be Father always and in everything, who lives his whole life in the Father's presence and love, who allows God in all the greatness of His love to be a Father to him, he will experience in a glorious way that a life that trusts in God's infinite fatherliness and continual answers to prayer are inseparable.

We begin to see why we know so little of daily answers to prayer and what the Lord's primary lesson is for us. It is rooted in the name of Father. Instead of new and deeper insight into some of the mysteries of the prayer-world as we expected, Christ tells us the highest lesson is to learn to say well, "Abba, Father!" and "Our Father which are in heaven." He who can say this has the key to all prayer. Consider the compassion with which a father listens to his weak or sickly child, the joy with which he hears his stammering child, the gentle patience with which he bears with a thoughtless child, and we study, as in so many mirrors, the heart of our Father. Then every prayer will be borne upward in faith in this word: "*How much more* shall your heavenly Father give good gifts to them that ask him."

Blessed Lord, we know so little of the love of the Father. Although this is one of the first, simplest, and most glorious lessons in your school, You know that it is one of the hardest to learn. Lord, teach us so to live with the Father that His love may be nearer, clearer, dearer to us than the love of any earthly father. And let the assurance of His hearing our prayer be as much greater than the confidence in an earthly parent, as the heavens are higher than earth, as God is infinitely greater than man. Lord, show us that only our unchildlike distance from the Father hinders the answer to prayer, and lead us on to the true life of God's children. Lord Jesus, we see that it is fatherlike love that awakens childlike trust. Reveal the Father, and His tender, pitying love to us that we may become childlike and experience the power of prayer that lies in the child-life.

Blessed Son of God, the Father loves you and has given you all things. And you love the Father, and have done all things He commanded you, and therefore have the power to ask all things. Lord, give us your own Spirit, the Spirit of the Son. Make us childlike, as you were on earth. And let every prayer be breathed in the faith that as the heaven is higher than the earth, so God's Father-love, and His readiness to give us what we ask, surpasses all we can think or conceive. Amen.

NOTE[1]

Your Father which is in heaven. Alas! we speak of it only as the utterance of a reverential homage. We think of it as a figure borrowed from an earthly life, and only in some faint and shallow meaning to be used of God. We are afraid to take God as our own tender and pitiful father. He is our schoolmaster, or almost farther off than that, and knowing less about us—an inspector, who knows nothing of us except through our lessons. His eyes are not on the scholar, but on the book, and all alike must come up to the standard.

Now open the ears of the heart, timid child of God; let it go sinking right down into the innermost depths of the soul. Here is the starting point of holiness, in the love and patience and pity of our heavenly Father. We are not to learn to be holy like a hard lesson at school, that we may make God think well of us; we are to learn it at home with the Father to help us. God loves you not because you are clever, not because you are good, but because He is *your Father*. The cross of Christ does not make God love us; it is the outcome and measure of His love to us. He loves all His children—the clumsiest, the dullest, the worst of His children. His love lies at the back of everything, and we must get upon that as the solid foundation of our religious life, not growing up into that, but growing up *out of it*. We must begin there or our beginning will come to nothing. Do take hold of this mightily. We must go out of ourselves for any hope, what strength, what confidence may be ours now that we begin here: *your Father which is in heaven!*

We need to get in at the tenderness and helpfulness which lie in these words, and to rest upon it—*your Father*. Speak them over to yourself until something of the wonderful truth is felt by us. It means that I am bound to God by the closest and tenderest relationship, that I have a right to His love and His power and His blessing, such as nothing else could give me. Oh, the boldness with which we can draw near! Oh, the great things we have a right to ask for! *Your Father*. It means that all His infinite love and patience and wisdom bend over *me* to help *me*. In this relationship lies not only the possibility of holiness but infinitely more.

Here we are to begin, in the patient love of our Father. Think how He knows us each in all our peculiarities, in all our weaknesses and difficulties. The master judges by the result, but our Father judges by the effort. Failure does not always mean fault. He knows how much things cost, and weighs them where others only measure. *Your Father.* Think how great store His love sets by the poor beginnings of the little ones, clumsy and unmeaning as they may be to others. All this and infinitely more lies in this blessed relationship. Do not fear to take it all as your own.

---

[1]From *Thoughts on Holiness* by Mark Guy Pearse. What is so beautifully said of the knowledge of God's fatherliness as the starting point of holiness is no less true of prayer.

LESSON SEVEN

The All-Comprehensive Gift

"If ye then, being evil, know how to give good gifts unto your children: how much more shall your heavenly Father give the Holy Spirit to them that ask him?" (Luke 11:13).

In the Sermon on the Mount, the Lord uttered His wonderful *"How much more?"* Here in Luke, where He repeats the question, there is a difference. Instead of speaking of giving *good gifts*, He says, "How much more shall the heavenly Father give *the Holy Spirit?"* He thus teaches us that the best of these gifts is the Holy Spirit, that in this gift all others are comprised. The Holy Spirit is the first of the Father's gifts and the one He delights most to bestow. The Holy Spirit is therefore the gift we ought to seek first.

The unspeakable worth of this gift we can easily understand. Jesus spoke of the Spirit as *"the* promise of the Father"—the one promise in which God's Fatherhood revealed itself. The best gift a good and wise father can bestow on a child on earth is his own spirit. To reproduce in his child his own disposition and character is the great object of a father in education. If the child is to know and understand his father and enter into all his will and plans, if he is to have his highest joy in the father and the father in him, the child must be of one mind and spirit with the father.

So it is impossible to conceive of God bestowing any higher gift on His child than His own Spirit. God is what He is through His Spirit. The Spirit is the very life of God. Think what it means—God giving His own Spirit to His child on earth.

Was not this the glory of Jesus as a Son upon earth, that the Spirit of the Father was in Him? At His baptism in Jordan the two things were united: the voice, proclaiming Him the Beloved Son, and the Spirit, descending upon Him. And so the apostle says of us, "Because ye are sons, God sent forth the Spirit of his Son into your hearts, crying, Abba, Father." A king seeks in the whole education of his son to call forth in him a kingly spirit. Our Father in heaven desires to educate us as His children for the holy, heavenly life in which He dwells. For this He gives us, from the depths of His heart, His own Spirit. This was Jesus' whole aim when, after having made atonement with His own blood, He entered into God's presence, to obtain for us, and send down to dwell in us, the Holy Spirit. As the Spirit of the Father and of the Son, the whole life and love of Father and Son are in Him. Coming down into us, He lifts us up into their fellowship. As Spirit of the Father, He sheds abroad the Father's love, with which He loved the Son, in our hearts, and teaches us to live in that love. As Spirit of the Son, He breathes into us the childlike liberty, devotion and obedience in which the Son lived on earth. The Father can bestow no higher or more wonderful gift than this—His own Holy Spirit, the Spirit of sonship.

This truth naturally suggests the thought that this first and best gift of God must be the first and main object of all prayer. For every need of the spiritual life the one thing needful is the Holy Spirit. All the fullness is in Jesus, the fullness of grace and truth, out of which we receive grace for grace. The Holy Spirit is the appointed instrument, whose special work it is to make Jesus—and all there is in Him for us—ours in personal appropriation and blessed experience. He is the Spirit of life in Christ Jesus. As wonderful as the life is so also is the provision by which such an agent is provided to communicate it to us. If we but yield ourselves entirely to the disposal of the Spirit and let Him have His way with us, He will manifest the life of Christ within us. He will do this with a divine power, maintaining the life of Christ in us in uninterrupted continuity. Surely, if there is one prayer that should draw us to the Father's throne and keep us there, it is for the Holy Spirit, whom we as children have received, to stream into us and out from us in greater fullness.

In the variety of the gifts which the Spirit has to dispense, He meets the believer's every need. Think of the names He bears. The Spirit of grace, to reveal and impart all of grace there is in Jesus. The Spirit of faith, teaching us to begin and go on and increase in believing. The Spirit of adoption and assurance, who witnesses that we are God's children, and inspires the confiding and confident "Abba, Father!" The Spirit of truth, to lead into all truth, and make each word of God ours in deed and in truth. The Spirit of prayer, through whom we speak with the Father in prayer that must be heard. The Spirit of judgment and burning, to search the heart and convince of sin. The Spirit of holiness, manifesting and communicating the Father's holy presence within us. The Spirit of power, through whom we are strong to testify boldly and work effectively in the Father's service. The Spirit of glory, the pledge of our inheritance, the preparation and the foretaste of the glory to come. Surely the child of God needs but one thing to be able really to live as a child: to be filled with this Spirit.

So Jesus teaches us that the Father is longing to give His Spirit to us if we will but ask in the childlike dependence on the promise, "If ye know how to give good gifts unto your children, *how much more* shall your heavenly Father give the Holy Spirit to them that ask Him." In God's promise, "I will pour out my Spirit *abundantly*," and His command, "Be ye *filled* with the Spirit," we see the measure of what God is ready to give and what we may obtain. As God's children we have already received the Spirit, but we still need to pray for His special gifts and operations as we require them. Not only this, but we need His unceasing momentary guidance. Just as the branch, even though filled with the sap of the vine, ever cries for the continued and increasing flow of the sap to bring its fruit to perfection, so the believer, rejoicing in the possession of the Spirit, ever thirsts and cries for more. Nothing less than God's promise and God's command should be the measure of our expectation and our prayer. We must be filled abundantly. Ask in the assurance that the wonderful *how much more* of God's Father-love is His pledge that, when we ask, we do most certainly receive.

When praying to be filled with the Spirit, do not look for the answer in feelings. All spiritual blessings must be accepted or taken in faith.[1] The Father *gives* the Holy Spirit to His praying child. Even as I pray, I should say in faith: "I have what I ask, the fullness of the Spirit is mine," and then continue steadfast in this faith. On the strength of God's Word we know that we have what we ask. So, with thanksgiving that we have been heard, with thanksgiving for what we have received and taken and now hold as ours, let us continue steadfast in believing prayer that the blessing, *which has already* been given us and which we hold in faith, may break through and fill our whole being. In such believing thanksgiving and prayer, our soul opens us for the Spirit to take entire and undisturbed possession. Such prayer not only asks and hopes, but takes and holds and inherits the full blessing. Remember, if there is one thing on earth we can be sure of, it is this: *The Father desires to have us filled with His Spirit and He delights to give us His Spirit.*

When once we have learned to believe this for ourselves, and each day to take out of the treasure we hold in heaven, what liberty and power there will be to pray for the outpouring of the Spirit on the Church of God, on all flesh, on individuals or their efforts! He that has once learned to know the Father in prayer for himself, learns to pray most confidently for others too. The Father gives the Holy Spirit to them that ask Him—not least but most—when they ask for others.

Father in heaven, you sent your Son to reveal yourself to us, your Father-love, and all that that love has for us. And He has taught us that the gift above all gifts which you would give in answer to prayer is the Holy Spirit.

My Father, I come to you with this prayer: there is nothing I desire so much as to be filled with the Holy Spirit. The blessings He brings are so unspeakable and just what I need. He sheds abroad your love in the heart and fills it with yourself. He breathes the mind and life of Christ into me so that I live as He did, in and for the Father's love. He endues with power from on high for all my walk and work. I long for all of this. Father, I beseech you to give me this day the fullness of your Spirit.

Father, I ask this, resting on the words of my Lord: "How much more the Holy Spirit." I do believe that you hear my prayer and I receive now what I ask. Father, I claim and take the fullness of your Spirit as mine. I receive the gift this day again as a faith gift. In faith I reckon my Father works through the Spirit all He has promised. The Father delights to breathe His Spirit into the waiting child who tarries in fellowship with Him. Amen.

---

[1]The Greek word for receiving and taking is the same. When Jesus said, "Every one that asketh *receiveth*," He used the same verb as at the Supper, "*Take*, eat," or on the resurrection morning, "*Receive*," accept, take, "the Holy Spirit." Receiving not only implies God's bestowment but also our acceptance.

The Boldness of God's Friends

"And he said unto them, Which of you shall have a *friend*, and shall go unto him at midnight, and say unto him, *Friend*, lend me three loaves; for *a friend* of mine in his journey is come to me and I have nothing to set before him? And he from within shall answer and say, Trouble me not: the door is now shut, and my children are with me in bed; I cannot rise and give thee. I say unto you, though he will not rise and give him because he is *his friend*, yet *because of his importunity* he will rise and give him as many as he needeth" (Luke 11:5-8).

The first teaching to His disciples was given by our Lord in the Sermon on the Mount. Almost a year later the disciples asked Jesus to teach them to pray. In answer He gave them the Lord's Prayer a second time, so teaching them *what* to pray. He then speaks of *how* they ought to pray, and repeats what He said before about God's fatherliness and the certainty of an answer. But in answer He adds the beautiful parable of the friend at midnight, to teach them the twofold lesson, that God wants us to pray not only for ourselves but also for the perishing around us, and that in such intercession great boldness of entreaty is often needed, and is always lawful and even pleasing to God.

The parable is a perfect storehouse of instruction about true intercession. First there is *the love* which seeks to help the needy around us: "*My friend* is come to me." Then *the need* which prompts the cry, "*I have nothing* to set before him." Then follows *the confidence* that help is to be had: "Which of you shall have *a friend*, and say, *Friend,* lend me three loaves." An unexpected *refusal* comes, "I *cannot* rise and give thee." But his *perseverance* takes no refusal: "because of his *importunity*." Last there comes the reward of such prayer: "he will give him *as many as he needeth*." This wonderfully illustrates the way of prayer and faith in which the blessing of God has so often been sought and found.

In the main thought of prayer as an appeal to the friendship of God, we find that two lessons are suggested. One, if we are God's friends, and come to Him as such, we must prove ourselves the friends of the needy. God's friendship to us and ours to others go hand in hand. The other is that we may use the utmost liberty in claiming an answer for our needy friends.

Prayer has a twofold use: one, to obtain strength and blessing of our own life; the other, the higher and the true glory of prayer, for which Christ has taken us into His fellowship and teaching, is intercession. There prayer is the royal power a child of God exercises in heaven on behalf of others and the kingdom. We see in Scripture, how in intercession for others Abraham and Moses, Samuel and Elijah, with all the holy men of old, proved that they had power with God and prevailed. When we give ourselves to be a blessing, then we can especially count on the blessing of God. When we draw near to God as the friend of the poor and the perishing, we may count on His friendliness. The righteous man who is the friend of the poor is a special friend of God. This gives wonderful liberty in prayer.

Lord, I have a needy friend whom I must help. As a friend I have undertaken to help him. In you I have a Friend whose kindness and riches I know to be infinite. I am sure you will give me what I ask. If I, being evil, am ready to do for my friend what I can, how much more will you, my heavenly Friend, do for your friend what he asks?

The question suggests itself as to whether the fatherhood of God does not give such confidence in prayer that the thought of His friendship can hardly teach us anything more because certainly a father is more than a friend. Still, this pleading the friendship of God opens new wonders to us. That a child obtains what he asks of his father looks so perfectly natural, we almost count it the father's duty to give. But with a friend it seems as if his kindness is more free and dependent, not on nature, but on sympathy and character. Another contrast is that the relation of a child is more that of perfect dependence, where two friends are more nearly on a level. So our Lord, in unfolding to us the spiritual mystery of prayer, shows His desire to have us approach God in this relation too—as those whom He has acknowledged as His friends, whose mind and life are in sympathy with His.

But for this we must be living as His friends. I am still a child even when a wanderer, but friendship depends upon conduct. "Ye are my friends if ye do whatsoever I command you." "Thou seest that faith wrought with his works, and by works was faith made perfect; and the scripture was fulfilled which saith, And Abraham believed God, and he was called *the friend of God*." It is *"the same* Spirit" that leads us that also bears witness to our acceptance with God.

"Likewise, also," the same Spirit helps us in prayer. Life as the friend of God gives the wonderful liberty to say: "I have a friend to whom I can go even at midnight." And how much more when I go in the very spirit of that friendliness, manifesting myself the very kindness I look for in God, seeking to help my friend as I want God to help me. When I come to God in prayer, He always looks for the motive behind my petition. If it be merely for my own comfort or joy I seek His grace, I do not receive. But if I can say that it is that He may be glorified in my dispensing His blessings to others, I shall not ask in vain. Or if I ask for others, but want to wait until God has made me so rich that it will involve no sacrifice or act of faith to aid them, I shall not obtain. But if I can say that I have already undertaken for my needy friend—that in my poverty I have already begun the work of love because I knew I had a friend who would help me—my prayer will be heard. We have no idea how much the plea avails where the friendship of earth looks in its need to the friendship of heaven: "He will give him as much as he needeth."

But not always at once. The one thing by which man can

honor and enjoy his God is *faith*. Intercession is part of faith's training school. There our friendship with men and with God is tested. Is my friendship with the needy so real that I will take time, sacrifice my rest and go even at midnight, and not cease until I have obtained for them what I need? Is my friendship with God so clear that I can depend on Him not to turn me away and therefore pray on until He gives?

What a deep heavenly mystery there is in persevering prayer. The God who has promised, who longs and whose fixed purpose it is to give the blessing, holds it back. It is to Him a matter of deep importance that His friends on earth should know and fully trust their rich Friend in heaven. For this reason He trains them, in the school of answer delayed, to find out how their perseverance really does prevail, and what the mighty power is they can wield in heaven, if they but set themselves to it. There is a faith that sees the promise, and embraces it and yet does not receive it (Heb. 11:13, 39). It is when the answer to prayer does not come and the promise we are most firmly trusting appears to be of no effect, that the trial of faith, more precious than of gold, takes place. In this trial the faith that has embraced the promise is purified, strengthened, and prepared by personal, holy fellowship with the living God to see His glory. Faith, then, takes and holds the promise until it receives the fullfillment of what was claimed as vital truth from the unseen but living God.

Each child of God working in love in his Father's service, take courage. Parents, teachers, preachers—all who have accepted and are bearing the burden of hungry, perishing souls—take courage. That God should really require persevering prayer, that there should be a real spiritual necessity for imporunity seems puzzling to us. To teach us, the Master uses this strange parable. If the unfriendliness of a selfish earthly friend can be conquered by importunity, how much more will it avail with the heavenly Friend, who loves to give, but is held back by our spiritual unfitness and our incapacity to possess what He has to give. Thank Him that by delaying His answer He is educating us up to our true position and the exercise of all our power with Him. He is training us to live with Him in the fellowship of undoubting faith and trust, to be indeed the friends of God. Let us hold fast the

threefold cord that cannot be broken:
1. The hungry friend needing the help,
2. The praying friend seeking the help,
3. The mighty Friend, loving to give as much as is needed.

My Blessed Lord and Teacher, I come to you in prayer. Your teaching is so glorious but it is too high for me to grasp. I confess that my heart is too small to comprehend these thoughts of the wonderful boldness I may use with your Father as my Friend. Lord Jesus, I trust you to give me your Spirit and your Word, and to make the Word quick and powerful in my heart. I desire to keep this Word: "Because of his importunity he will give him as many as he needeth."

Lord, teach me to know more of the power of persevering prayer. I see that the Father knows our need of time for the inner life to attain its growth and ripeness, so that His grace may indeed be assimilated and made our very own. I know that He wants to train us to exercise a strong faith that does not let Him go even in the face of seeming disappointment. I know He wants to lift us to that wonderful liberty in which we understand how really He has made the dispensing of His gift dependent on our prayer. Lord, I say I know this, but teach me to really understand it in spirit and truth.

Now may it be my joy to act as agent for my rich Friend in heaven and care for all the hungry and perishing—even at midnight. I can do this in confidence because I know my Friend always gives to him who perseveres, because of his importunity, as much as he needs. Amen.

LESSON NINE

Prayer Provides Laborers

"Then saith he unto his disciples, The harvest truly is plenteous but the labourers are few. Pray ye therefore the Lord of the harvest, that he will send forth labourers into his harvest" (Matt. 9:37-38).

The Lord frequently taught His disciples that they *must* pray, and *how*, but seldom *what* to pray. This He left to their sense of need and the leading of the Spirit. But here we have one thing He expressly commands them to remember. In view of the abundant harvest and the need of reapers, they must cry to the Lord of the harvest to send forth laborers. Just as in the parable of the friend at midnight, He wants them to understand that prayer is not to be selfish. It is the power through which blessing can come to others. The Father is Lord of the harvest, so when we pray for the Holy Spirit, we must pray for Him to prepare and send out laborers for the work.

Strange, is it not, that He should ask His disciples to pray for this? Could He himself not pray? Would not one prayer of His accomplish more than a thousand of theirs? Did not God, the Lord of the harvest, see the need? Would He not, in His own good time, send forth laborers—even without the disciples praying? Such questions lead us to the deepest mysteries of prayer, and its power in the Kingdom of God. Answers to such questions convince us that prayer is indeed a power on which the ingathering of the harvest and the coming of the Kingdom truly depend.

Prayer is no empty form or show. The Lord Jesus was truth. Everything He spoke was the deepest truth. When (see v. 36) "he saw the multitude, and was moved with compassion on them, because they were scattered abroad, as sheep having no shepherd," He called on the disciples to pray for laborers to be sent among them. He did so because He really believed that their prayer would help and was needed. The veil which hides the invisible world from us was wonderfully transparent to the holy human soul of Jesus. He had looked long and deep and far into the hidden connection of cause and effect in the spirit world. He showed from God's Word how, when God called men like Abraham, Moses, Joshua, Samuel, and Daniel, and gave them authority over men in His name, He at the same time gave them the authority and right to call the powers of heaven to their aid as needed. He knew that, just as the work of God had been entrusted to these men of old, and to himself for a time here upon earth, so now it was about to pass into the hands of His disciples. He knew that when this work should be given over to them, it would not be mere form or show. Instead the success of the work would actually depend on them, whether they were faithful or unfaithful. As a single individual within the limitations of a human body and a human life, Jesus feels how little a short visit can accomplish among these wandering sheep He sees around Him. He longs for help to have them properly cared for. So He tells His disciples to pray—both now and when they have taken over the work from Him on earth—as one of the chief petitions in their prayer, that the Lord of the harvest himself would send forth laborers into His harvest. The God who entrusted them with the work, and made it so largely dependent on them, gives them authority to appeal to Him for laborers to help, and makes the supply dependent on their prayer.

How little Christians really feel and mourn the need of laborers in the fields of the world so white to the harvest. How little they believe that our labor supply depends on prayer and that prayer will really provide "as many as he needeth." It is not that the dearth of labor is not known or discussed, nor that efforts are not sometimes put forth to supply the want. But how little the burden of the sheep wandering without a Shepherd is really carried in faith that the Lord of the harvest *will* send forth laborers in answer to prayer. There is no solemn conviction that without this prayer fields ready for reaping will be left to perish. But these are vital truths.

So wonderful is the surrender of His work into the hands of His Church, so dependent has the Lord made himself on them as His body through whom alone His work can be done, so real is the power which the Lord gives His people to exercise in heaven and earth, that the number of the laborers and the measure of the harvest does actually depend upon their prayer.

Solemn thought! Why do we not obey the injunction of the Master more heartily and cry more earnestly for laborers? There are two reasons. One, we lack the compassion of Jesus which gave rise to this request for prayer. When believers learn that the Father's first commandment to His redeemed ones is to love their neighbors as themselves and to live entirely for God's glory in their fellow men, they will accept the care and concern for these perishing ones as the charge entrusted to them by their Lord. In accepting them not only as a field of labor but also as objects of loving care and interest, before long compassion toward the hopelessly perishing will touch their heart and the cry ascend with an earnestness before unknown: "Lord! Send laborers."

The other reason for neglect of the command, want of faith, will then be revealed, but it can be overcome as our pity pleads for help. We believe too little in the power of prayer to bring about definite results. We do not live close enough to God, and are not enough entirely given up to His service and Kingdom, to be capable of the confidence that He will give this faith in answer to our prayer. Pray for a life so one with Christ that His compassion may stream into us and His Spirit give assurance that our prayers will be answered.

Such prayer will ask and obtain a double blessing. First there will be the desire for an increase in men entirely given up to the service of God. It is a terrible blot upon the Church of Christ that at times men simply cannot be found to serve the Master as ministers, missionaries, or teachers of God's Word. As God's children pray for this for their own circle or Church, men will be given. The Lord Jesus is now Lord of the harvest. He has been exalted to bestow gifts—the gifts of the Spirit. His chief gifts are men filled with the Spirit. But the supply and distribution of these gifts depend on the cooperation of Head and members. Only prayer will lead to such cooperation. Then those who pray will plead for men and means for the work.

The other blessing to be asked is no less important. Every believer is a laborer. Every one of God's children has been redeemed for service and has his work waiting. Our prayer should be that the Lord will so fill all His people with a spirit of dedication that not one may be found standing idle in the vineyard. Wherever there is complaint of a lack of workers or of competent helpers for God's work, prayer holds the promise for them to be supplied. There is no work for God where He is not ready and able to provide. It may take time and importunity, but Christ's command to ask the Lord of the harvest is the pledge that the prayer will be heard: "I say unto you, he will arise and give him as many as he needeth."

It is a solemn, blessed thought that this prayer has been given to us to provide for the world's need and to obtain helpers for God's work. The Lord of the harvest will hear. Christ, who called us especially to pray in this way will support our prayers offered in His name and interest. Let us set apart time and give ourselves to this part of our intercessory work. It will lead us into the fellowship with His compassionate heart that led Him to call for our prayers. It will elevate us to an insight into our regal position as those whose will counts for something with the great God in the advancement of His Kingdom. It will make us feel how truly we are God's fellow workers on earth. A share in His work has in downright earnest been entrusted to us. It will make us partakers not only in the soul travail, but also in the soul satisfaction of Jesus, as we see how blessing has been given in answer to our prayer that otherwise would not have come.

Blessed Lord, again this day you have given us another of your wonderful lessons to learn. We humbly ask you to help us see clearly the spiritual realities of which you have been speaking. The harvest is so large—and perishing—as it waits for sleepy disciples to give the signal for laborers to come. Lord, teach us to look out upon it with a heart moved with compassion and pity. The laborers are so few. Lord, show us how terrible is the sin of the lack of prayer and faith of which this is the token. The Lord of the harvest is so able and ready to send them forth. Lord, show us how He does indeed wait for the prayer to which He has bound His answer. There are the disciples, to whom the commission to pray has been given. Lord, show us how you can pour down your Spirit and breathe upon them, so your compassion and the faith in your promise will rouse them to unceasing, prevailing prayer.

Lord, we do not understand how you trust such work and give such power to men so slothful and unfaithful. We thank you for all whom you are teaching to cry day and night for laborers to be sent forth. Lord, breathe your own Spirit on all your children that they may learn to live for this one thing alone—the Kingdom and glory of their Lord—and become fully awake to faith in what their prayer can accomplish. Fill our hearts with the assurance that prayer, offered in loving faith in the living God, will bring certain and abundant answer. Amen.

LESSON TEN

Prayer Must be Definite

"And Jesus answered and said unto him, What wilt thou that I should do unto thee?" (Mark 10:51).

The blind man had been crying out over and over, "Thou Son of David, have mercy on me." The cry reached the ear of the Lord who knew what the man wanted, and Jesus was ready to give it to him. But first Jesus asks, "*What wilt thou* that I should do unto thee?" Jesus wants to hear from the man's own lips, not only the general petition for mercy, but the distinct expression of his desire. Until he declares that, he is not healed.

There is now still many a praying person to whom the Lord puts the same question, and who cannot, until it has been answered, get the aid he asks. Our prayers must not be a vague appeal to His mercy or an indefinite cry for blessing, but the distinct expression of definite need. It is not that Jesus' loving heart does not understand our cry or is not ready to hear, but He desires us to be specific for our own good. Definite prayer teaches us to know our own needs better. To find out what really is our greatest need demands time, thought, and self-scrutiny. To find whether our desires are honest and real, such as we are ready to persevere in, searches us and puts us to the test. It leads us to judge whether our desires conform to God's Word, and whether we really believe that we shall receive the things we ask. It helps us to wait for the definite answer, and to be aware of it when it comes.

And yet how much of our prayer is vague and pointless. Some cry for mercy, but without specifying why they need mercy. Others ask, perhaps, to be delivered from sin, but do not begin by naming any sin from which the deliverance may be claimed. Still others pray for God's blessing on those around them, for the outpouring of God's Spirit on their land or the world, and yet do not pinpoint a particular spot where they wait and expect to see God answer. To all, the Lord asks: "What is it you really want and expect Me to do?"

Every Christian has only limited powers, and as he must have his own special field of labor in which he works, so his prayers encompass a particular group too. Each believer has his own circle, his family, his friends, his neighbors. If he were to take one or more of these by name, he would find that this really brings him into the training school of faith, and leads to personal and pointed dealing with his God. When in such specific matters we have in faith claimed and received answers, then our more general prayers will be believing and effective.

We all know with what surprise the whole civilized world heard of the way in which trained troops were repulsed by the Transvaal Boers at Majuba. And to what did they owe their success? In the armies of Europe the soldier fires upon the enemy standing in large masses, and never thinks of seeking an aim for every bullet. In hunting game, the Boer had learned a different lesson: his practiced eye knew to send every bullet on its special mission to seek and find its man. Such aiming works in the spiritual world too.

As long as in prayer we just pour out our hearts in a multitude of requests without taking time to see whether each one is sent with the purpose and expectation of getting an answer, not many will reach the mark. But if, as in silence of soul we bow before the Lord, we were to ask such questions as these: What is my real desire? Do I ask for it with faith, expecting to receive? Am I ready to place it—and leave it—in the Father's keeping? Is it settled between God and me that I will receive the answer? We should learn to pray so that God would see and we would know what we really expect.

This is one reason that the Lord warns us against the vain repetitions of the Gentiles, who think to be heard for their much praying. We often hear prayers of great earnestness and fervor, in which a multitude of petitions are poured forth, but to which the Saviour would undoubtedly answer, "What will you have Me do for you?"

In a strange land on business for my father, I would certainly write two different types of letters. There would be family letters, affectionate and newsy, and there would be business letters, containing orders for what I needed. And there might be letters combining both types of news. The answers would correspond to the letters. To each sentence of the letters containing the family news, I would not expect a special answer. But for each order I sent, I would be confident of an answer as to whether the desired article had been forwarded. This business element must also be present in our dealings with God. Along with our expression of need and sin, of love and faith and consecration, there must be a pointed statement of what we ask and expect to receive. In that kind of answer, the Father loves to show us His approval and acceptance.

But the word of the Master teaches us more. He does not say, "What do you *want*?" but, "What do you *will*?" One often wants something without willing it. I want to have a certain article, but I find the price too high; I resolve not to take it. I *want* but do not *will* to have it. The sluggard wants to be rich but does not will it. Many a person wants to be saved but is lost because he does not will it. The will rules the whole heart and life. If I really will to have anything that is within my reach, I do not rest until I have it. So, when Jesus asks us, "What will you have?" He asks whether we purpose indeed to have what we ask at any price no matter how great the sacrifice. Do we so will to have our request that, even though He delays the answer for a long time, we do not rest until He hears? It is sad that many prayers are merely wishes, sent up for a short time and then forgotten, or sent up year after year as matter of duty, while we remain content with the prayer without the answer.

But is it not best to make our wishes known to God and then let Him decide what is best, without seeking to assert our will? By no means. This is the very essence of the prayer of faith, to which Jesus sought to train His disciples that it does not only make known its desire and then leave the decision to God. That would be the prayer of submission for those cases in which we cannot know God's will. But the prayer of faith, finding God's will in some promise of the Word, pleads for that until it is given. In Matthew 9:28 we read that Jesus asked the blind man, "*Believe ye* that I can do this?" Here in Mark He asks, "*What wilt thou* that I should do?" In both cases He said that faith had saved them. So He said to the Syrophenician woman, "Great is thy *faith*: be it unto thee even as thou *wilt*." Faith is nothing but the purpose of the will resting on God's word and saying: "I must have this." To believe truly is to will firmly.

But does such a will contradict our dependence on God and our submission to Him? By no means. Rather, it is the true submission that honors God. It is only when the child has yielded his own will in entire surrender to the Father that he receives from the Father liberty and power to will what he would have. But, when the will of God, as revealed through the Word and Spirit, has been accepted by the believer as his will, too, then the will of God is that His child should use this renewed will in His service. The will is the highest power in the soul. Grace wants above everything to sanctify and restore this will—one of the chief traits of God's image—to full and free exercise. As a son who only lives for his father's will is trusted by the father with his business, so God speaks to His child in all truth, "What wilt thou?" Often spiritual sloth under the guise of humility professes to have no will, because it fears the trouble of searching out the will of God, or the struggle of claiming it in faith when found. True humility is always coupled with strong faith, which only seeks to know the will of God, and then boldly claims fulfillment of the promise: "Ye shall ask *what ye will*, and it shall be done unto you."

Lord Jesus, teach me to pray with all my heart and strength so clearly that there may be no doubt as to what I have asked.

May I know what it is that I desire so that when my petitions are recorded in heaven, I can record them on earth too, and note each answer when it comes. And may my faith in what your Word has promised be so clear that the Spirit may indeed work in me the liberty to will that it shall come. Lord, renew, strengthen, and sanctify wholly my will for the work of effective prayer.

Blessed Saviour, reveal to me the wonderful condescension you show us by asking us to say what we will that you should do, and promising to do whatever we will. Son of God, I cannot understand it. I can only believe that you have indeed redeemed us wholly for yourself and are seeking to make the will—our noblest part—your most efficient servant. Lord, I yield my will unreservedly to you, as the power through which your Spirit is to rule my whole being. Let Him take possession of it, lead it into the truth of your promises, and make it so strong in prayer that I may ever hear your voice saying: "Great is your faith. Be it unto you even as you will." Amen.

The Faith that Takes

"Therefore I say unto you, All things whatsoever ye pray and ask for, believe that ye have received them, and ye shall have them" (Mark 11:24).

What a promise—so large, so divine, that our limited understanding cannot take it in. In every possible way we seek to limit it to what we think safe or probable; instead of allowing it just as He gave it, in all its quickening power and energy, to enter in and enlarge our hearts to the measure of what His love and power are really ready to do for us. Faith is very far from being a mere conviction of the truth of God's word or a conclusion drawn from certain premises. It is the ear which has heard God say what He will do, the eye which has seen Him doing it. Therefore, where there is true faith, the answer *must* come. If we only do the one thing that He asks of us as we pray: "Believe *that ye have received*," He will do the thing He has promised: *"Ye shall have them."* The keynote of Solomon's prayer in 2 Chron. 6:4, "Blessed be the Lord God of Israel, who hath *with his hands fulfilled* that which *he spake with his mouth* to my father David," is the keynote of all true prayer—the joyful adoration of a God whose *hand* always secures the fulfillment of what His *mouth* hath spoken. In this spirit let us listen to the promise Jesus gives; each part of it has its divine message.

"All things whatsoever." At this first word our human wisdom at once begins to doubt and ask, "Surely this cannot be literally true?" But if it is not, why did the Master say it and use the strongest expression He could find: "All things whatsoever." It is not as if this were the only time He spoke this way—He also said, "If thou canst believe, *all things* are possible to him that believeth" and "If ye have faith, *nothing* shall be impossible to you." Faith is so wholly the work of God's Spirit through His Word in the prepared heart of the believing disciple that it is impossible that the fulfullment should not come. Faith is the pledge and forerunner of the coming answer. Yes, "*All things whatsoever* ye shall ask in prayer *believing, ye receive.*" The tendency of human reason is to interpose here certain qualifying clauses—"if expedient," "if according to God's will"—to break the force of a statement which appears dangerous. Beware of dealing this way with the Master's words. His promise is literally true. He wants His often-repeated *"all things"* to penetrate our hearts and reveal how mighty the power of faith is and how wholly our Father shares His power and places it at the disposal of the child that wholly trusts Him. Faith is to have its food and strength in this "all things"; if we weaken this, we weaken faith. The *whatsoever* is unconditional. The only condition is what is implied in the believing. Before we can believe, we must determine God's will with certainty. Believing is the exercise of a soul surrendered to the influence of the Word and the Spirit. When once we do believe, nothing shall be impossible. God forbid that we should try to bring down His *"all things"* to the level of what we think possible. Let us now simply take Christ's *"whatsoever"* as the measure and the hope of our faith; it is a seed-word which, if taken just as He gives it, and kept in the heart, will open and take root, fill our life with its fullness and bring forth much fruit.

"All things whatsoever *ye pray and ask for.*" In prayer these *all things* are to be brought to God, to be asked and received of Him. The faith that receives them is the fruit of the prayer. In one aspect there must be faith before there can be prayer; in another, faith is the outcome and the growth of prayer. In the personal presence of the Saviour, and fellowship with Him, faith rises to grasp what at first appeared too high. In prayer we hold

up our desire to the light of God's holy will, our motives are tested, and proof given whether we ask indeed in the name of Jesus
and only for the glory of God. In prayer we wait for the leading of
the Spirit to show us whether we are asking the right thing in the
right spirit. In prayer we become conscious of our want of faith.
We are led on to tell the Father that we do believe, and we prove
the reality of our faith by the confidence with which we persevere. In prayer Jesus teaches and inspires faith. He that waits to
pray, or who loses heart in prayer because he does not yet feel the
faith needed to get the answer, will never learn to believe. He
who begins to pray and ask will find the Spirit of faith is given
nowhere so surely as at the foot of the throne.

"*Believe* that ye have received." Clearly, what we are to believe is that we receive the very things we ask. The Saviour does
not even hint that because the Father knows what is best, He
may give us something else. The very mountain that faith bids
depart is cast into the sea. There is a prayer in which, in everything, we make known our requests with prayer and supplication, and the reward is the sweet peace of God keeping heart and
mind. This is the prayer of trust. It has reference to things that
we cannot find out if God is going to give them. As children we
make known our desires in the countless things of daily life, and
leave it to the Father to give or not as He thinks best. But the
prayer of faith of which Jesus speaks is something different,
something higher. When, in the Master's work or in our daily life,
the soul sees that nothing so honors the Father as the faith that
He will do what He has said—give us whatsoever we ask for—and
then takes its stand on that promise as brought home by the
Spirit, it may know most certainly that it does receive exactly
what it asks. The Lord sets this clearly before us in verse 23:
"Whosoever shall not doubt in his heart, but shall believe that
what he saith cometh to pass, he shall have it." This is the blessing of the prayer of faith of which Jesus speaks.

"Believe that ye *have received*." In this word of central importance, the meaning is too often misunderstood. Believe that
you have received the thing you ask for—now, while praying.
Maybe only later you shall have it in personal experience and
you shall see what you believe; but now, without seeing, you are

to believe that it has been given to you by the Father in heaven. The receiving or accepting of an answer to prayer is just like the receiving or accepting of Jesus or of pardon—a spiritual thing, an act of faith apart from all feeling. When I come to ask pardon, I believe that Jesus in heaven is for me, and so I receive or take Him. When I come to ask any special gift according to God's Word, I believe that what I ask is given me. I believe that I have it, I hold it in faith. I thank God that it is mine. "If we know that he heareth us, whatsoever we ask, we know that we have the petitions which we have asked of Him."

"And ye shall have them." That is, the gift which we first hold in faith as bestowed upon us in heaven will also become ours in personal experience. But will it be necessary to pray longer if once we know we have been heard and have received that for which we asked? Sometimes such prayer will not be needful, in cases where the blessing is ready to break through at once, if we but hold fast our confidence and prove our faith by praising for what we have received in the face of our not yet having it in experience. In other cases, the faith that has received needs to be still further tried and strengthened in persevering prayer. God alone knows when everything in and around us is fully ripe for the manifestation of the blessing that has been given to faith. Elijah knew for certain that rain would come—God had promised it— and yet he had to pray the seven times. But that prayer was no show or play; it was an intense spiritual reality in the heart of him who lay pleading there, and in heaven above where it had work to do. Through faith *and patience* we inherit the promises. Faith says most confidently, "I have received it." Patience perseveres in prayer until the gift bestowed in heaven is seen on earth. "Believe that *ye have received*, and *ye shall have.*" Between the *have received* in heaven, and the *shall have* on earth is the link— believing praise and prayer.

Remember, it is Jesus who said this. As we see heaven thus opened to us, and the Father on the throne offering to give us whatsoever we ask in faith, our hearts feel full of shame that we have availed ourselves so little of our privilege. We are full of fear lest our feeble faith still fail to grasp what is so clearly placed within our reach. One thing strengthens and gives hope: it is

Jesus who has brought us this message from the Father. He himself, when He was on earth, lived the life of faith and prayer. When the disciples expressed their surprise at what He had done to the fig tree, He told them that the very same life He led could be theirs; they could not only command the fig tree, but the very mountain, and it must obey. He is our life. All He was on earth He is in us now. All He teaches He really gives. He himself is the author and the perfecter of our faith. He gives the spirit of faith. Such faith is meant for us. It is meant for every child of the Father. It is within reach of each one who will but be childlike, yielding himself to the Father's will and love, trusting the Father's word and power. The thought that this word comes through Jesus, the Son, our Brother, encourages us to answer: "Blessed Lord, we do believe your word. We do believe that we receive."

Blessed Lord, you came from the Father to show us all His love and all the treasures of blessing that love is waiting to bestow. You have this day again flung the gates so wide open, and given us such promises as to our liberty in prayer that we must blush that our poor hearts have taken in so little. It has been too big for us to believe.

Lord, we now look up to you to teach us to take and keep and use this precious word of yours: "All things whatsoever ye ask, believe that ye have received." Blessed Jesus, our faith must be rooted in you if it is to grow strong. Your work has freed us wholly from the power of sin, and opened the way to the Father. Your love is ever longing to bring us into the full fellowship of your glory and power. Your Spirit is ever drawing us upward into a life of perfect faith and confidence. We are assured that in your teaching we shall learn to pray the prayer of faith. You will train us to pray so that we believe that we receive, to believe that we really have what we ask.

Lord, teach me so to know and trust and love you, so to live and abide in you, that all my prayers rise up and come before God in you, and that my soul may have in you the assurance that I am heard. Amen.

The Secret of Believing Prayer

"And Jesus answering saith unto them, Have faith in God. For verily I say unto you, That whosoever shall say unto this mountain, Be thou removed, and be thou cast into the sea; and shall not doubt in his heart, but shall believe that those things which he saith shall come to pass; he shall have whatsoever he saith. Therefore I say unto you, What things soever ye desire, when ye pray, believe that ye receive them, and ye shall have them" (Mark 11:22-24).

The promise of answer to prayer is one of the most wonderful lessons in all Scripture. But in how many hearts has it raised the question: "How can I ever attain the faith that knows that it will receive all it asks?"

Our Lord answers this question. Before He gave that wonderful promise to His disciples, He told where faith in the answer to prayer begins and always receives its strength. Have faith in God: this word precedes the other where He said to have faith in the promise of an answer to prayer. The power to believe a promise depends entirely on faith in the one who made the promise. Trust in the person arouses trust in his word. Only when we live with God in a personal, loving relationship where God himself is everything to us, only when our whole being is continually opened up and exposed to the mighty working of His holy presence within, is a capacity developed to believe that He gives whatsoever we ask.

This connection between faith in God and faith in His promise becomes clear to us if we think what faith really is. Often it is compared to the hand or the mouth by which we take and appropriate what is offered to us. But is is important to understand that faith is also the ear by which I hear what is promised, the eye by which I see what is offered to me. On this the power to take depends. I must *hear* the person who gives me the promise. The very tone of his voice gives me courage to believe. I must *see* him. In the light of his eye and countenance, all fear as to my right to take fades away. The value of the promise depends on the one who made the promise. It is on my knowledge of his character that faith in the promise depends. For this reason before Jesus gives that wonderful prayer-promise, He first says, "Have faith in God." That is, let your eye be open to and gaze on the living God, seeing Him who is invisible. Through the eye I yield myself to the influence of what is before me. I allow it to enter, exert its influence, and leave its impression on my mind. So believing God is just looking to God and what He is, allowing Him to reveal His presence, giving Him time and yielding the whole being to fully comprehend what He is as God. Believing, the soul opens to receive and rejoice in the overshadowing of His love. Faith is the eye to which God shows what He is and does. Through faith the light of His presence and the workings of His mighty power stream into the soul. As that which I see lives in me, so by faith God lives in me too.

Faith is also the ear through which the voice of God is heard and intimacy with Him maintained. Through the Holy Spirit the Father speaks to us. The Son is the Word, the substance of what God says. The Spirit is the living voice. The child of God needs this to lead and guide him. The secret voice from heaven must teach him, as it taught Jesus, what to say and what to do. An ear opened toward God, a believing heart waiting on Him to hear what He says, will hear Him speak. The words of God will not only be the words of a Book, but because they proceed from the mouth of God, they will be spirit and truth, life and power. They will transform into deed and living experience what are otherwise only thoughts. Through this opened ear the soul waits under the influence of the life and power of God himself. As the words I hear enter the mind and dwell and work there, so through faith God enters the heart to dwell and work there.

When faith is in full exercise as eye and ear, as the faculty of the soul by which we see and hear God, it will be able to exercise its full power as hand and mouth, by which we appropriate God and His blessings. The power of reception will depend entirely on the power of spiritual perception. For this reason before Jesus gave the promise that God would answer believing prayer, He said, "Have faith in God." Faith is simply surrender. By faith *I yield myself to the living God* because of what I hear and learn about Him. His glory and love fill my heart and master my life. Faith is fellowship. I give myself up to the influence of the friend who makes me a promise and become linked to him by it. When we enter into this living fellowship *with God himself* in a faith that always sees and hears Him, it becomes easy and natural to believe His promise as to prayer. Faith in the promise is the fruit of faith in the one who promised. The prayer of faith is rooted in the life of faith. So faith that prays effectively is indeed a gift of God—not as something that He bestows or infuses at once, but in a far deeper and truer sense, as the blessed attitude or habit of soul which grows in us during a life of communion with Him. Surely one who knows his Father well, and lives in constant close fellowship with Him, finds it a simple thing to believe the promise that the Father will do the will of His child who lives with him in close union.

It is because very many of God's children do not understand this connection between the life of faith and the prayer of faith that their experience of the power of prayer is so limited. When they earnestly desire to obtain an answer from God, they fix their whole heart upon the promise, and try their utmost to grasp that promise in faith. When they do not succeed, they are ready to give up hope. The promise is true but it is beyond their power to take hold of it in faith.

Jesus teaches: Have faith in God, the living God. Let faith look to God more than toward the thing promised. God's love, power, and His living presence will awaken and build up faith.

To one asking for some means to get more strength in his arms and hands to be able to seize and hang on to things, a physician would say that his whole constitution must be built up and strengthened. So the cure of a feeble faith is only found by revitalizing our whole spiritual life through close fellowship with God. Learn to believe in God, take hold of God, let God take possession of your life, and it will be easy to take hold of the promise. He who knows and trusts God finds it easy to trust the promise too.

This is demonstrated clearly in the saints of old. Every special exhibition of the power of faith was the fruit of a special revelation of God. See it in Abraham: *"And the word of the Lord came unto Abram, saying, Fear not, Abram; I am thy shield. And he brought him forth abroad, and said . . . And he believed the Lord."* Later: *"The Lord appeared unto him, and said unto him, I am God, Almighty. And Abram fell on his face, and God talked with him, saying, As for me, behold my covenant is with thee."* The revelation of God himself gave the promise its living power to enter the heart and build faith.

Because they knew God, these men of faith trusted His promise. God's promise will be to us what God himself is. The man who walks before the Lord and falls upon his face to listen while the living God speaks to him will be the one who will really receive the promise.

Though we have God's promises in the Bible and full liberty to take them, the spiritual power is lacking unless God himself speaks them to us. And He speaks to those who walk and live with Him. Therefore, have faith in God: let faith be all eye and ear, then surrender to let God reveal himself fully in the soul. Count it one of the chief blessings of prayer to exercise faith in God as the living mighty God who waits to fulfill in us all the good pleasure of His will and the work of faith with power. See Him as the God of Love, whose delight is to bless and impart himself. In such worship of faith in God, the power will speedily grow to believe His promise: "All things whatsoever ye ask, believe that ye receive." In faith make God your own; then the promise will be yours also.

Jesus teaches us that, although we seek God's gifts, God

wants to give us himself first. We think of prayer as the power to draw down good gifts from heaven; Jesus, as the means to draw ourselves up to God. We want to stand at the door and cry but Jesus would have us first enter in and realize that we are friends and children. Let us accept the teaching. Let every experience of the littleness of our faith in prayer urge us to have and exercise more faith in the living God, and then in such faith to yield ourselves to Him. A heart full of God has power for the prayer of faith. Faith in God begets faith in the promise—in the promise too of an answer to prayer.

Therefore, child of God, take time, take time, to bow before *Him*, to wait on *Him* to reveal *himself*. Take time to let your soul in holy awe and worship exercise and express its faith in the Infinite One. As He imparts himself and takes possession of you the prayer of faith will crown your faith in God.

O my God, I do believe in you. I believe in you as the Father, infinite in your love and power; and as the Son, my Redeemer and my Life; and as the Holy Spirit, Comforter and Guide and Strength. Three-One God, I have faith in you. I know and am sure that all that you are, you are to me, that all you have promised you will perform.

Lord Jesus, increase this faith. Teach me to take time, to wait and worship in the holy presence until my faith takes in all there is in my God for me. Let it see Him as the fountain of all life, working with almighty strength to accomplish His will in the world and in me. Let it see Him in His love longing to meet and fulfill my desires. Let it so take possession of my heart and life that through faith God alone may dwell there. Lord Jesus, help me! With my whole heart I want to believe in God. Let faith in God each moment fill me.

O my blessed Saviour, how can your Church glorify you, how can it fulfill that work of intercession through which your kingdom must come unless our whole life be faith in God. Speak that word into the depths of our souls. Amen.

The Cure of Unbelief

"Then came the disciples to Jesus apart, and said, Why could not we cast him out? And Jesus said unto them, *Because of your unbelief:* for verily I say unto you, *If ye have faith* as a *grain of mustard seed . . . nothing shall be impossible* to you. Howbeit this kind goeth not out but *by prayer and fasting*" (Matt. 17:19-21).

When the disciples saw Jesus cast the evil spirit out of the epileptic whom they could not cure, they asked the Master for the cause of their failure. He had given them power and authority over all devils, and to cure all diseases. They had often exercised that power and joyfully told how the devils were subject to them. But now, while He was on the Mount, they had utterly failed. That there had been nothing in the will of God or in the nature of the case to render deliverance impossible had been proved. At Christ's bidding the evil spirit had gone out.

From their question, "Why could we not?" it is evident that they had wished and tried to do so. They had probably used the Master's name and called upon the evil spirit to go out. Their efforts had been in vain and in the presence of the multitude, they had been put to shame. "Why could we not?"

Christ's answer was direct and plain: "Because of your unbelief." The cause of His success and their failure was not due to

His having a special power to which they had no access. No, the reason was not hard to find. He had so often taught them that there is one power—faith—to which in the kingdom of darkness, as well as in the kingdom of God, everything must bow. In the spiritual world failure has but one cause, the lack of faith.

Faith is the one condition on which all divine power can enter into man and work through him. It is the acceptance of the unseen: man's will yielded up to, and molded by the will of God. The power they had received to cast out devils, they did not hold in themselves as a permanent gift or possession. The power was in Christ, to be received and held and used by faith alone, living faith in Him. Had they been full of faith *in Him* as Lord and Conqueror in the spirit world, had they been full of faith *in Him* as having given them authority to cast out in His name, this faith would have given them the victory. "Because of your unbelief" was, for all time, the Master's explanation and reproof of impotence and failure in His Church.

But lack of faith must have a cause too. The disciples might well have asked: "And why could we not believe? Our faith has cast out devils before this. Why have we now failed in believing?" The Master proceeds to tell them before they ask: "This kind goeth not out but by fasting and prayer."

As faith is the simplest, so it is the highest exercise of the spiritual life, where our spirit yields itself in perfect receptivity to God's Spirit, and so is strengthened to its highest activity. This faith depends entirely upon the state of the spiritual life. Only when this is strong and in full health, when the Spirit of God has full sway in our life, is there the power of faith to do its mighty deeds. Therefore Jesus adds: "Howbeit this kind goeth not out but by fasting and prayer."

The faith that can overcome such stubborn resistance as you have just seen in this evil spirit, Jesus tells them, is not possible except to men living in very close fellowship with God, and in very special separation from the world—in prayer and fasting. And so He teaches us two lessons about prayer of deep importance. The one, faith needs a life of prayer in which to grow and keep strong. The other, prayer needs fasting for its full and perfect development.

Faith needs a life of prayer for its full growth. In all the different parts of the spiritual life, there is such close union, such unceasing action and reaction, that each may be both cause and effect. That is true with faith also. There can be no true prayer without faith. Some measure of faith must precede prayer. Prayer is also the way to more faith. There can be no higher degrees of faith except through much prayer. This is the lesson Jesus teaches here.

Nothing needs to grow as much as our faith. "Your faith groweth exceedingly" is said of one church. When Jesus said, "According to your faith be it unto you," He announced the law of the kingdom, which tells us that all have not equal degrees of faith, that the same person has not always the same degree, and that the measure of faith must always determine the measure of power and of blessing. If we want to know where and how our faith is to grow, the Master points us to the throne of God. In prayer, in the exercise of the faith I have, in fellowship with the living God, faith can increase. Faith can live only by feeding on what is divine, on God himself.

It is in the adoring worship of God, the waiting on Him and for Him, the deep silence of soul which yields itself for God to reveal himself, that the capacity for knowing and trusting God will be developed. As we take the Book, bring it to Him and ask Him to speak His word to us with His living, loving voice, that power will come fully to believe and receive the word as God's own word to us. It is in prayer, in living contact with God in living faith, that faith—the power to trust God, and in that trust, to accept everything He says, to accept every possibility He has offered to our faith—will become strong in us.

Many Christians cannot understand what is meant by the much prayer they sometimes hear spoken of. They feel no need and cannot conceive of spending hours with God. But what the Master says and what the experience of His people has confirmed is that men of strong faith are men of much prayer.

This brings us again to Jesus' first lesson, "Have faith in God." Our faith must strike its roots deep and broad into the living God; then that faith will be strong to remove mountains and cast out devils. "If ye have faith, nothing shall be impossible to you."

If we give ourselves to the work God has for us in the world—coming into contact with the mountains and the devils there are to be cast away and cast out—we soon comprehend the need there is of much faith, and of much prayer as the only soil in which faith can be cultivated.

Christ Jesus is our life and the life of our faith too. It is His life in us that makes us strong, and makes us simple to believe. In the dying to self which much prayer implies, in closer union to Jesus, the spirit of faith will come in power. *Faith needs prayer* for its full growth.

Prayer needs fasting for its full growth. This is the second lesson. Prayer is the one hand with which we grasp the invisible; fasting, the other, with which we let loose and cast away the visible. In nothing is man more closely connected with the world of sense than in his need of food and his enjoyment of it. It was the fruit, good for food, with which man was tempted and fell in Paradise. When Jesus was hungry in the wilderness, it was with bread to be made from stones that He was tempted, and in fasting that He triumphed. The body has been redeemed to be a temple of the Holy Spirit; it is in body as well as spirit, Scripture says, in eating and drinking, we are to glorify God. There are many Christians to whom this eating to the glory of God has not yet become a spiritual reality. The first thought suggested by Jesus' words about fasting and prayer is that only in a life of moderation and temperance and self-denial will there be the heart or the strength to pray much.

But there is also a more literal meaning. Sorrow and anxiety cannot eat. Joy celebrates in feasts with eating and drinking. There may come times of eating and drinking. There may come times of intense desire, when it is strongly felt that the body and its appetites—lawful though they be—still hinder the spirit in its battle with the powers of darkness, and the need is felt of keeping it under. We are creatures of the senses. Our mind is helped by what comes to us embodied in concrete form. Fasting helps to express, to deepen, and to confirm the resolution, that we are ready to sacrifice anything to attain what we seek for the kingdom of

God. And He who accepted the fasting and sacrifice of the Son knows to value and accept and reward with spiritual power the soul that is ready in this way to give up all for Christ and His kingdom.

A still wider application follows. Prayer is reaching out after God and the unseen; fasting is letting go of all that is of the seen and temporal. Ordinary Christians imagine that all that is not positively forbidden and sinful is lawful to them and seek to retain as much as possible of this world, with its property, its literature, its enjoyments. In contrast, the truly consecrated soul is as the soldier who carries only what he needs for the warfare. Laying aside every weight and easily besetting sins, afraid of entangling himself with the affairs of this life, he seeks to lead a Nazarite life, as one especially set apart for the Lord and His service. Without such voluntary separation—even from what is lawful— no one will attain power in prayer. *This kind goeth not out but by fasting and prayer.*

Disciples of Jesus, who have asked the Master to teach you to pray, come now and accept His lessons. He tells you that prayer is the path to faith, strong faith, that can cast out devils. He tells you: "If ye have faith, nothing shall be impossible to you." Let this glorious promise encourage you to pray much. Is the prize not worth the price? Shall we not give up all to follow Jesus in the path He opens to us here? Shall we not, if need be, fast? Shall we not do anything so that neither the body nor the world around hinder us in our great life-work—having an intimate relationship with our God in prayer, so that we may become men of faith whom He can use in His work of saving the world?

Lord Jesus, how continually you have to reprove us for our unbelief! How strange it must appear to you, this terrible incapacity for trusting our Father and His promises. Lord! let your reproof, with its searching, "Because of your unbelief," sink into the very depths of our hearts, and reveal to us how much of the sin and suffering around us we are guilty of. Then teach us, blessed Lord, that there is a place where faith can be learned and obtained—in prayer and fasting that brings us into living and abiding fellowship with you and the Father.

O Saviour, you yourself are the author and the Perfecter of our faith. Teach us to let you live in us by your Holy Spirit. Lord, our efforts and prayers for grace to believe have been so unavailing. We know why—we looked for strength in ourselves that is given by you. Teach us the mystery of your life in us, and how, by your Spirit, you undertake to live in us the life of faith and to see to it that our faith shall not fail. Show us that our faith will only be a part of that wonderful prayer life which you give those who expect to be trained for the ministry of intercession, not only in word and thought but also in the holy anointing you give, the inflowing of the Spirit of your own life. Teach us how, in fasting and prayer, we may grow up to the faith to which nothing shall be impossible. Amen.

NOTE

At the time when Blumhardt was passing through his terrible conflict with the evil spirits in those who were possessed, and seeking to cast them out by prayer, he often wondered what it was that hindered the answer. One day a friend, to whom he had spoken of his trouble, directed his attention to our Lord's words about fasting. Blumhardt resolved to give himself to fasting, sometimes for more than thirty hours. From reflection and experience, he gained the conviction that it is of more importance than is generally thought. He says, "Inasmuch as the fasting is before God a practical proof that the thing we ask is to us a matter of true and pressing interest, and inasmuch as in a high degree it strengthens the intensity and power of the prayer, and becomes the unceasing practical expression of a prayer without words, I could believe that it would not be without efficacy, especially as the Master's words had reference to a case like the pres-

ent. I tried it, without telling anyone, and in truth the later conflict was extraordinarily lightened by it. I could speak with much
greater restfulness and decision. I did not require to be so long
present with the sick one; and I felt that I could influence without
being present."

LESSON FOURTEEN

Prayer and Love

"And when ye stand praying, forgive, if ye have aught against any; that your Father also which is in heaven may forgive you your trespasses" (Mark 11:25).

These words follow the promise, "All things whatsoever ye pray, believe that ye have received them, and ye shall have them." Before that, "Have faith in God" taught us that for effective prayer all depends upon our relation to God being clear. Now these words remind us that our relation with fellowmen must be clear too. Love to God and love to our neighbor are inseparable. Prayer from a heart that is not right—either with God on the one side, or with men on the other—cannot prevail. Faith and love are essential to each other.

Our Lord frequently gave expression to this thought. When speaking about the sixth commandment, He taught His disciples that acceptable worship of the Father was impossible if everything were not right with the brother. "If thou art offering thy gift at the altar, and there rememberest that thy brother hath aught against thee, leave there thy gift before the altar, and go thy way; first be reconciled to thy brother, and then come and offer thy gift." (Matt. 5:23, 24). Later He taught us to pray, "Forgive us our debts, as we also have forgiven our debtors." Then at the

81

close of the prayer, He added: "If you forgive not men their trespasses, neither will your Father forgive your trespasses." At the close of the parable of the unmerciful servant, He applies His teaching, "So shall also my heavenly Father do unto you, if you forgive not every one his brother from your hearts."

Now, beside the dried-up fig tree, He speaks of the wonderful power of faith and the prayer of faith. All at once—apparently without connection—He introduces the thought, "When ye stand praying, forgive, if ye have aught against any one; that your Father also which is in heaven may forgive you your trespasses." Apparently, during His life at Nazareth and afterward, the Lord had learned that disobedience to the law of love to men was the great sin even of praying people, and the great cause of the weakness of their prayer. He now wants to lead us into His own blessed experience that nothing gives such liberty of access and such power in believing as the consciousness that we have given ourselves in love and compassion for those whom God loves.

The first lesson taught here is that of a forgiving disposition. We pray, "Forgive, *even as* we have forgiven." Scripture says, "Forgive one another, even as God also in Christ forgave you." God's full and free forgiveness is to be our rule with men. Otherwise our reluctant, halfhearted forgiveness, which is not forgiveness at all, will be God's rule with us. Every prayer rests upon our faith in God's pardoning grace. If God dealt with us after our sins, not one prayer could be heard.

Pardon opens the door to all God's love and blessing. Because God has pardoned all our sin, our prayer can prevail to obtain all we need. The deep, sure ground of answer to prayer is God's forgiving love. When it possesses our heart, we pray in faith, we also live in love. God's forgiving disposition, revealed in His love to us, becomes our disposition. As the power of His forgiving love penetrates our heart and dwells within us, we forgive even as He forgives. If there is great and grievous injury or injustice done to us, we try first of all to possess a godlike disposition; to be kept from a sense of wounded honor, from a desire to maintain our rights, or from rewarding the offender as he deserves.

In the little annoyances of daily life, we are watchful not to excuse the hasty temper, the sharp word, and the quick judgment, with the thought that we mean no harm, that we do not stay angry for long, or that it would be too much to expect from weak human nature that we should really forgive the way God and Christ do. No, we take the command literally, "*Even as* Christ forgave, *so also* do ye." The blood that cleanses the conscience from dead works cleanses from selfishness too. The love it reveals is pardoning love that takes possession of us and flows through us to others. Our forgiving love to men is the evidence of the reality of God's forgiving love in us, and so it is a condition for the prayer of faith.

There is a second, more general lesson: our daily life in the world is the test of our relationship with God in prayer. How often the Christian, when he comes to pray, does his utmost to cultivate certain frames of mind which he thinks will be pleasing. He does not understand, or forgets, that life does not consist of so many loose pieces, of which first one and then another can be taken up. Life is a whole. The pious frame of the hour of prayer is judged by God from the total frame of the ordinary daily life of which the hour of prayer is but a small part. Not the feeling I muster up, but the tone of my life during the day, is God's criterion of what I really am and desire. My drawing near to God is one with my relationship with men and earth; failure here will cause failure there. Not only the distinct consciousness of anything wrong between my neighbor and myself, but also the ordinary current of my thinking and judging, or unloving thoughts and words I allow to pass unnoticed, can hinder my prayer. The effective prayer of faith comes from a life surrendered to the will and the love of God. My prayer is dealt with by God not according to what I try to be when praying, but what I am when not praying.

These thoughts form a third lesson. In our life with men the one thing on which everything depends is love. The spirit of forgiveness is the spirit of love. Because God is love, He forgives. Only when we are dwelling in love can we forgive as God forgives. In love for the brethren we have the evidence of love for the Father, the ground of confidence before God, and the assurance that our prayer will be heard.

Let us love in deed and truth; *hereby* shall we assure our heart before Him. If our heart condemn us not, we have boldness toward God, and whatever we ask, we receive of Him. Neither faith nor work will profit if we have not love. It is love that unites with God. Love proves the reality of faith. As essential as in the word that precedes the great prayer-promise in Mark 11:24, "Have faith in God," is this one that follows it, "Have love to men." Right relations, both to the living God above me and with the living men around me, are conditions of effective prayer.

This love is of special consequence when we labor and pray for them. We sometimes work for Christ, from zeal for His cause or for our own spiritual health, without giving ourselves in personal self-sacrificing love for those whose souls we seek. No wonder that our faith is feeble and does not conquer.

To look on each wretched one, no matter how unlovable, in the light of the tender love of Jesus the Shepherd seeking the lost; to see Jesus Christ in him, and for Jesus' sake to take him up with a heart that really loves—this is the secret of believing prayer and successful effort. In speaking of forgiveness Jesus speaks of love as its root. In the Sermon on the Mount, He connected His teaching and promises about prayer with the call to be merciful as the Father in heaven is merciful (Matt. 5:7, 9, 22, 38-48), and again here we see that a loving life is the condition of believing prayer.

Nothing is so heart-searching as believing prayer, or even the honest effort to pray in faith. Let us not blunt the edge of that self-examination by the thought that God does not hear our prayer for reasons known to himself alone. By no means. "Ye ask and receive not, because ye ask amiss." Let that word of God search us.

Is our prayer indeed the expression of a life wholly given over to the will of God and the love of man? Love is the only soil in which faith can put down roots and thrive. As it throws its arms up and opens its heart heavenward, the Father always looks to see if it has them opened toward the evil and the unworthy too. In that love—not of perfect attainment but the love of fixed purpose and sincere obedience—faith alone can obtain the blessing. He who gives himself to let the love of God dwell in him, and in the practice of daily life to love as God loves, will have the power to believe in the Love that hears his every prayer. It is *the Lamb,* who is in the midst of the throne; it is suffering and forbearing love that prevails with God in prayer. The merciful shall obtain mercy. The meek shall inherit the earth.

Blessed Father, you are Love, and only he who abides in love abides in you and in fellowship with you. The blessed Son has this day again taught me how deeply true this is in my fellowship with you in prayer. Oh, my God! let your love, planted in my heart by the Holy Spirit, be in me a fountain of love to all around me, that out of a life in love may spring the power of believing prayer. Oh, my Father, grant by the Holy Spirit that this may be my experience, that a life in love to all around me may be the gate to a life in the love of my God. Especially help me to find in the joy with which I forgive day by day whoever might offend me, the proof that your forgiveness to me is a power and a life.

Lord Jesus, my blessed teacher, teach me to forgive and to love. Let the power of your blood make the pardon of my sins such a reality, that forgiveness, as shown by you to me, and by me to others, may be the very joy of heaven. Show me whatever in my relationship with fellowmen might hinder my fellowship with God, so that my daily life in my own home and in society may be the school in which strength and confidence are gathered for the prayer of faith. Amen.

The Power of United Prayer

"Again I say unto you, That if two of you shall agree on earth as touching any thing that they shall ask, *it shall be done* for them of my Father which is in heaven. For where two or three are gathered together in my name, there am I in the midst of them" (Matt. 18:19, 20).

One of the first lessons our Lord taught about prayer was: Not to be seen of men. Enter an inner room. Get alone with the Father. When He has taught us that prayer means personal, individual contact with God, He comes with a second lesson: You need not only secret and solitary but also public, united prayer. He gives a very special promise for the united prayer of two or three who agree in what they ask. For its full development, a tree has its root hidden in the ground and its stem growing up into the sunlight. In the same way prayer equally needs both the hidden secrecy in which the soul meets God alone and the public fellowship with those who find in the name of Jesus their common meeting place.

The reason why this must be so is plain. The bond that unites a man to his fellowmen is no less real and close than that which unites him to God: he is one with them. Grace renews our relation not only to God but also to man. We learn to say not only

"My Father," but "Our Father." Nothing would be more unnatural than for the children of a family to always meet their father separately, but never in the united expression of their desires or their love. Believers are members not only of one family but of one body. Just as each member of the body depends on the other, and the full action of the spirit dwelling in the body depends on the union and cooperation of all, so Christians cannot reach the full blessing God is ready to give through His Spirit unless they seek and receive it in fellowship with each other. In the union and fellowship of believers, the Spirit can manifest His full power. It was to the hundred and twenty continuing in one place together, and praying with one accord, that the Spirit came from the throne of the glorified Lord.

The marks of true united prayer are given us in these words of our Lord. The first is *agreement* as to the thing asked. There must be not only a general consent to agree with anything another may ask, but also some special matter of distinct united desire; as in all prayer, the agreement must be in spirit and in truth. In such agreement it will become very clear to us exactly what we are asking and whether we may confidently ask according to God's will, and whether we are ready to believe that we have received what we ask.

The second mark concerns the gathering together in the name of Jesus. Later we shall learn much more of the need and the power of the name of Jesus in prayer; here our Lord teaches us that the name must be the center of union for believers, the bond that unites them into one, just as a home contains and unites all who are in it.

"The name of the Lord is a strong tower; the righteous runneth into it and escape." That name is such a reality to those who understand and believe it, that to meet in it is to have the Lord himself present. The love and unity of His disciples attract Jesus. "Where two or three are gathered in my name, *there am I in the midst of them.*" The living presence of Jesus, in the fellowship of His loving, praying disciples, gives united prayer its power.

The third mark is the sure answer: "It shall be done for them

of my Father." A prayer meeting for maintaining religious fellowship or seeking our own edification may have its use; but this was
not the Saviour's view in its appointment. He meant it as a
means of securing *special answer to prayer*. A prayer meeting
without recognized answer to prayer ought to be an anomaly.
When any of us have distinct desires in regard to which we feel
too weak to exercise the needful faith, we ought to seek strength
in the help of others. In the unity of faith, of love and of the
Spirit, the power of the name and the presence of Jesus acts more
freely and the answer comes more surely. The mark that there
has been true united prayer is the fruit—the answer and receiving of the thing we have asked: "I say unto you, *It shall be done*
for them of my Father which is in heaven."

What an unspeakable privilege united prayer is and what a
power it might be:

1. If the believing husband and wife knew that they were
joined together in the name of Jesus to experience His presence
and power in united prayer (1 Peter);

2. If friends believed what mighty help two or three praying
together could give each other;

3. If in every prayer meeting the coming together in His
name, faith in His presence, and the expectation of the answer
were of foremost importance;

4. If in every church united, effective prayer were regarded as
one of the chief purposes for which they are banded together and
the highest exercise of their power as a church;

5. If in the Church universal the coming of the kingdom, the
coming of the King himself, first in the mighty outpouring of His
Holy Spirit, then in His own glorious person, were really matters
of unceasing united crying to God—

Who can say what blessing might come to, and through, those
who agreed in this way to prove God in the fulfillment of His
promise.

In the Apostle Paul we see very distinctly what a reality his
faith in the power of united prayer was. To the Romans he writes
(15:30): "I beseech you, brethren, by the love of the Spirit, that
ye *strive together with me* in your prayers to God for me." In answer, he expects to be delivered from his enemies and to be pros-
pered in his work.

To the Corinthians (2 Cor. 1:11), "God will still deliver us, ye also helping together on our behalf by your supplications," their prayer is to have a real share in his deliverance.

To the Ephesians he writes: "With all prayer and supplication praying at all seasons in the Spirit for all the saints and on my behalf, that utterance may be given unto me." His power and success in his ministry depend on their prayers.

With the Philippians (1:19), he expects that his trials will turn to his salvation and the progress of the gospel *through your supplications and* the supply of the Spirit of Jesus Christ."

To the Colossians (4:3) he adds to the injunction to continue steadfast in prayer: "Withal praying for us too, that God may open unto us a door for the word."

And to the Thessalonians (2 Thess. 3:1) he writes: "Finally, brethren, pray for us, that the word of the Lord may run and be glorified, and that we may be delivered from unreasonable men."

Everywhere it is evident that Paul felt himself the member of a body, on whose sympathy and cooperation he was dependent. He counted on the prayers of these churches to obtain for him what otherwise might not be given. The prayers of the Church were to him as real a factor in the work of the kingdom as the power of God.

Who can say what power a church could develop and exercise, if it gave itself to the work of prayer day and night for the coming of the kingdom, for God's power on His servants and His word, for the glorifying of God in the salvation of souls?

Most churches think their members are gathered into one simply to take care of and build up each other. They know not that God rules the world by the prayers of His saints; that prayer is the power by which Satan is conquered; that by prayer the church on earth has disposal of the powers of the heavenly world. They do not remember that by His promise Jesus has consecrated every assembly in His name to be a gate of heaven, where His presence is to be felt, and His power experienced in the Father fulfilling their desires.

We cannot sufficiently thank God for the blessed week of united prayer, with which Christendom in our days opens every year. It is of unspeakable value as proof of our unity and our faith in the power of united prayer. It trains us to enlarge our hearts to take in all the needs of the Church universal and helps toward united persevering prayer. But especially as a stimulus to continued union in prayer in the smaller circles, its blessing has been great. It will become even greater, as God's people recognize what it is for all to meet as one in the name of Jesus; as they have His presence in the midst of a body all united in the Holy Spirit and boldly claim the promise that what they agree to ask shall be done of the Father.

Blessed Lord, in your high-priestly prayer you asked so earnestly for the unity of your people. Now teach us how you invite and urge us to this unity by your precious promise about united prayer. When we are one in love and desire our faith has your presence and the Father's answer.

Father, we pray for your people, and for every smaller circle of those who meet together, that they may be one. Remove all selfishness and self-interest, all narrowness of heart and estrangement which hinder that unity. Cast out the spirit of the world and the flesh through which your promise loses all its power. Let the thought of your presence and the Father's favor draw us all nearer to each other.

Grant especially, blessed Lord, that your Church may believe that by the power of united prayer she can bind and loose in heaven; that Satan can be cast out; that souls can be saved; that mountains can be removed; that the kingdom can be hastened. And grant, Lord, that in the circle with which I pray, the prayer of the Church may indeed be the power through which your name and Word are glorified. Amen.

The Power of Persevering Prayer

"And he spake a parable unto them to this end that men ought always to pray, and not to faint . . . And the Lord said, Hear what the unrighteous judge saith. And shall not God avenge his own elect, which cry to him day and night, and he is long-suffering over them? I say unto you, that he will avenge them speedily" (Luke 18:1, 6-8).

Of all the mysteries of the prayer world, the need of persevering prayer is one of the greatest. We cannot easily understand that the Lord, who is so loving and longing to bless, should have to be asked time after time, sometimes year after year, before the answer comes. This is also one of the greatest practical difficulties in the exercise of believing prayer. After persevering supplication, when your prayer remains unanswered, it is often easiest for our slothful flesh—with the appearance of pious submission—to think that we must now cease praying, because God may have His secret reason for withholding His answer to our request.

By faith alone the difficulty is overcome. When once faith has taken its stand upon God's Word and the name of Jesus, and has yielded itself to the leading of the Spirit to seek only God's will and honor in its prayer, it need not be discouraged by delay. It knows from Scripture that the power of believing prayer is simply irresistible. Real faith can never be disappointed.

To exercise the irresistible power it can have, faith, just like water, must be gathered up and accumulated until the stream can come down in full force. Often there must be a heaping up of prayer until God sees that the measure is full and the answer comes. Just as the plowman has to take his ten thousand steps and sow his ten thousand seeds, each one a part of the preparation for the final harvest, so there is a need for oft-repeated persevering prayer, all working out some desired blessing. It knows for certain that not a single believing prayer can fail of its effect in heaven, but each has its influence, and is treasured up to work toward an answer in due time to him who perseveres to the end.

Faith knows that it deals, not with human thoughts or possibilities, but with the word of the living God. Just as Abraham through so many years "in hope believed against hope," and then "through faith *and patience* inherited the promise," faith believes that the long-suffering of the Lord is salvation, *waiting for* the coming of its Lord to fulfill His promise.

To enable us to combine quiet patience and joyful confidence in our persevering prayer, when the answer to our prayer does not come at once, we need especially to understand the two words in which our Lord sets forth the character and conduct, not of the unjust judge, but of our God and Father, toward those whom He allows to cry day and night to Him: "He is *long-suffering* over them . . . he will avenge them *speedily*."

He will avenge them *speedily*, the Master says. The blessing is all prepared. He is not only willing but most anxious to give them what they ask. Everlasting love burns with the longing desire to reveal itself fully and satisfy the needs of its beloved. God will not delay one moment longer than is absolutely necessary. He will do all in His power to hasten and speed the answer.

But if this be true and His power be infinite, why does the answer to prayer often delay so long? Why must God's own elect so often, in the midst of suffering and conflict, cry day and night?

"He is *long-suffering* over them." Behold! the husbandman waiteth for the precious fruit of the earth, being *long-suffering* over it, till it receive the early and the latter rain." The husbandman does indeed long for his harvest, but knows that it must have its full time of sunshine and rain, and so has much patience. A child so often wants to pick the half-ripe fruit; the husbandman knows to wait until the proper time. Man, in his spiritual nature, too, is under the law of gradual growth that reigns in all created life. Only in the path of development can he reach his divine destiny. And it is the Father, in whose hands are the times and seasons, who alone knows the moment when the soul or the Church is ripened to that fullness of faith in which it can really take and keep the blessing. As a father longs to have his only child home from school, but still waits patiently until the time of training is completed, so it is with God and His children. He is the long-suffering One and answers speedily.

Insight into this truth leads the believer to cultivate corresponding attitudes. *Patience* and *faith, waiting* and *hastening,* are the secret of his perseverance. By faith in God's promise, we know that we *have* the petitions we have asked of Him. Faith takes hold of the answer in the promise, as an unseen spiritual possession, then rejoices and praises for it.

But there is a difference between the faith that thus holds the word and knows that it has the answer, and the clearer, fuller, riper faith that claims the promise as a present experience. It is in persevering, not unbelieving, but confident and praising prayer, that the soul grows up into that full union with its Lord in which it can enter upon the possession of the blessing in Him. Before the answer can fully come there may be things that have to be put right through our prayer—in those around us, in that great system of being of which we are part or in God's government—but the faith that has, according to the command, believed that it has received, can allow God to take His time. It knows it has prevailed and must prevail. In quiet, persistent, and determined perseverance, it continued in prayer and thanksgiving until the blessing comes. So we see combined what at first sight appears contradictory—faith that rejoices in the answer from the unseen God as a present possession, along with the patience that cries day and night until it be revealed. The *speedily* of God's *long-suffering* is met by the triumphant but patient faith of His waiting child.

Our great danger in this school of the answer delayed is the temptation to think that, after all, it may not be God's will to give us what we ask. If our prayer be according to God's Word and under the leading of the Spirit, let us not give way to these fears. Let us learn to give God time. God needs time with us. If we only give Him time—in daily fellowship with him—for Him to exercise the full influence of His presence on us, and time—day by day, in the course of our being kept waiting—for faith to prove its reality and to fill our whole being, then He himself will lead us from faith to vision. We shall see the glory of God.

Let no delay shake our faith. Faith also yields—first the blade, then the ear, then the full corn in the ear. Each believing prayer brings the final victory a step nearer. Each believing prayer helps to ripen the fruit and bring it nearer; fills up the measure of prayer and faith known to God alone; conquers the hindrances in the unseen world; hastens the end. Child of God, give the Father time. He is long-suffering over you. He wants the blessing to be rich, and full and sure. Give Him time, while you cry day and night. Only remember the word: "I say unto you, he will avenge them speedily."

The blessing of such persevering prayer is unspeakable. Nothing is so heart-searching as the prayer of faith. It teaches you to discover and confess, and give up everything that hinders the coming of the blessing and everything that may not be in accordance with the Father's will. It creates a closer fellowship with Him who alone can teach to pray. It leads to a more entire surrender, to draw near under no covering but that of the blood and the Spirit. It calls to a closer and more simple abiding in Christ alone. Christian, give God time. He will perfect that which concerns you. "Long-suffering—speedily" is God's watchword as you enter the gates of prayer. Let it be yours too.

Let it be this way whether you pray for yourself or for others. All labor, bodily or mental, needs time and effort. We must give *ourselves* to it. Nature reveals her secrets and yields her treasures only to diligent and thoughtful labor. However little we can understand it, in spiritual husbandry it is the same: the seed we sow in the soil of heaven, the efforts we put forth and the influence we seek to exert in the world above, need our whole being—we must *give ourselves* to prayer. But let us hold fast the confidence that in due season we shall reap if we faint not.

Remember this lesson as we pray for the Church of Christ. She is indeed like the poor widow who, in the absence of her Lord is apparently at the mercy of her adversary and unable to obtain help. Let us, when we pray for His Church or any portion of it under the power of the world, ask Him to visit her with the mighty workings of His Spirit and to prepare her for His coming. Let us pray with assured faith that prayer does help, praying always and not fainting will bring the answer. Only give God time. Then keep crying day and night. "Hear what the unrighteous judge saith. And shall not God avenge his own elect, which cry to him day and night, and *he is long-suffering* over them? I say unto you, that *he will avenge them speedily.*"

O Lord my God, teach me to know your way, and in faith to grasp what your beloved Son has taught: "He will avenge them speedily." Let your tender love, and the delight you have in hearing and blessing your children, lead me to accept implicitly your promise that we receive what we believe, that we have the petitions we ask, and that in due time the answer will be seen.

Lord, help us understand the seasons in nature, and know to wait with patience for the fruit we long for. Fill us with the assurance that you will not delay one moment longer than is needed, and that faith will yield the answer.

Blessed Master, you have said that it is a sign of God's elect that they cry day and night. Teach us to understand this. You know how speedily we grow faint and weary. It seems as if the Divine Majesty is so much beyond the need or the reach of continued supplication that it is improper for us to be too importunate. Lord, teach me how real the labor of prayer is. Here on earth, when I have failed in an undertaking, I can often succeed by renewed and more continuing effort, by giving more time and thought: show me how, by giving myself completely to prayer and to live more in prayer, I shall obtain what I ask. Above all, blessed Teacher, Author and Perfecter of faith, by your grace let my whole life be one of faith in the Son of God who loved me and

gave himself for me—in whom my prayer is accepted, in whom I
have the assurance of the answer, from whom the answer will be
mine. Lord Jesus, in this faith I will pray always and not faint.
Amen.

NOTE

The need of persevering, importunate prayer appears to some
to be at variance with the faith which knows that it has received
what it asks (Mark 11:24). One of the mysteries of the divine life
is the harmony between the gradual and the sudden, immediate
full possession and slow, imperfect appropriation. So here persevering prayer appears to be the school in which the soul is
strengthened for the boldness of faith. With the diversity of operations of the Spirit there may be some in whom faith takes more
the form of persistent waiting; to others, triumphant thanksgiving appears the only proper expression of the assurance of having
been heard.

In a very remarkable way the need of persevering prayer, and
the gradual rising into greater ease in obtaining answer, is illustrated in the life of Blumhardt. Complaints had been lodged
against him of neglecting his work as a minister of the gospel and
devoting himself to the healing of the sick, and especially his un-
authorized healing of the sick belonging to other congregations.
In his defense he writes: "I simply ventured to do what becomes
one who has the charge of souls, and to pray according to the
command of the Lord in James 1:6, 7. In no way did I trust to my
own power, or imagine that I had any gift that others had not.
But this is true, I set myself to the work as a minister of the gospel, who has a right to pray. But I speedily discovered that the
gates of heaven were not fully open to me. Often I was inclined to
retire in despair. But the sight of the sick ones, who could find
help nowhere, gave me no rest. I thought of the word of the Lord:
'Ask, and it shall be given you' (Luke 11:9, 10). And further, I
thought that if the Church and her ministers had, through unbelief, sloth, and disobedience, lost what was needed for the over-
coming of the power of Satan, it was just for such times of
leanness and famine that the Lord had spoken the parable of the

friend at midnight and his three loaves. I felt that I was not worthy thus at midnight, in a time of great darkness, to appear before God as His friend, and ask for a member of my congregation what he needed. And yet, to leave him uncared for, I could not either. And so I kept knocking, as the parable directs, or, as some have said, with great presumption and tempting God. Be this as it may, I could not leave my guest unprovided. At this time the parable of the widow became very precious to me. I saw that the Church was the widow, and I was a minister of the Church. I had the right to be her mouthpiece against the adversary; but for a long time the Lord would not. I asked nothing more than the three loaves; what I needed for my guest. At last the Lord listened to the importunate beggar, and helped me. Was it wrong of me to pray thus? The two parables must surely be applicable somewhere, and where was greater need to be conceived?

"And what was the fruit of my prayer? The friend who was at first unwilling, did not say, 'Go now; I will myself give to your friend what he needs; I do not require you'; but gave it to me as His friend, to give to my guest. And so I used the three loaves, and had to spare. But the supply was small, and new guests came; because they saw I had a heart to help them, and that I would take the trouble even at midnight to go to my friend. When I asked for them, too, I got the needful again, and there was again to spare. How could I help that the needy continually came to my house? Was I to harden myself, and say, 'Why do you come to me? There are larger and better homes in the city, go there.' Their answer was, 'Dear sir, we cannot go there. We have been there: they were very sorry to send us away so hungry, but they could not undertake to go and ask a friend for what we wanted. Do go, and get us bread, for we suffer great pain.' What could I do? They spoke the truth, and their suffering touched my heart. However much labor it cost me, I went each time again, and got the three loaves. Often I got what I asked much quicker than at first, and also much more abundantly. But all did not care for this bread, and so some left my home hungry."[1]

In his first struggles with the evil spirits, it took him more than eighteen months of much prayer and labor before the final victory was gained. Afterward he had such ease of access to the throne, and stood in such close communication with the unseen world, that often when letters came asking prayer for sick people, he could, after just looking upward for a single moment, obtain the answer as to whether they would be healed.

---

[1]From *Johann Christophe Blumhardt, Ein Lebensbild von F. Zündel.*

Prayer in Harmony with the Being of God

"Father, I thank thee that thou hast heard me. And I knew that thou hearest me always" (John 11:41, 42).

"Thou are my Son; this day have I begotten thee. Ask of me, and I shall give thee. . . " (Ps. 2:7, 8).

In the New Testament we find a distinction made between faith and knowledge. "To one is given, through the Spirit, the word of *wisdom*; to another the word of *knowledge*, according to the same Spirit; to another *faith*, in the same Spirit." In a child or a childlike Christian there may be much faith with little knowledge. Childlike simplicity accepts the truth without difficulty, and often cares little to give itself or others any reason for its faith but this: God has said. But it is the will of God that we should love and serve Him, not only with all the heart but also with all the mind; that we should grow up into an insight into the divine wisdom and beauty of all His ways and words and works. Only by growing this way will the believer be able fully to approach and rightly adore the glory of God's grace. Only in that way can our heart intelligently comprehend the treasures of wisdom and knowledge there are in redemption, and be prepared to enter fully into the highest note of the song that rises before the throne: "Oh the depth of the riches both of the wisdom and knowledge of God!"

This truth has its full application in our prayer life. While prayer and faith are so simple that the new-born convert can pray with power, the doctrine of prayer presents deep problems. Is the power of prayer a reality? How can God grant to prayer such mighty power? How can the action of prayer be harmonized with the will and the decrees of God? How can God's sovereignty and our will, God's liberty and ours, be reconciled? These and other similar questions are valid subjects for Christian meditation and inquiry. The more earnestly and reverently we approach such mysteries, the more we shall fall down in adoring awe to praise Him who has in prayer given such power to man.

One of the secret difficulties with regard to prayer is one which though not expressed, often really does hinder prayer. This difficulty is derived from the perfection of God, in His absolute independence of all that is outside of himself. Is He not the Infinite Being, who owes what He is to himself alone, who determines himself, and whose wise and holy will has determined all that is to be? How can prayer influence Him, or He be moved by prayer to do what otherwise would not be done? Is not the promise of an answer to prayer simply a condescension to our weakness? Is what is said of the power—the much-availing power—of prayer anything more than an accommodation to our mode of thought, because the Deity never can be dependent on any action from without for its doings? Is not the blessing of prayer simply the influence it exercises upon ourselves?

In seeking an answer to such questions, we find the key in the very being of God, in the mystery of the Holy Trinity. If God was only one person, shut up within himself, there could be no thought of nearness to Him or influence on Him. But in God there are three persons. In God we have Father and Son, who have in the Holy Spirit their living bond of unity and fellowship. When eternal Love begat the Son, and the Father gave the Son as the second person a place next to himself as His equal and His counselor, there was a way opened for prayer and its influence in the very inmost life of Deity itself.

Just as on earth, so in heaven the whole relation between Father and Son is that of giving and taking. And if that taking is to be as voluntary and self-determined as the giving, there must be on the part of the Son an asking and receiving. In the holy fellowship of the divine persons, this asking of the Son was one of the great operations of the thrice-blessed life of God. We see it in Psalm 2: "This day have I begotten thee. Ask of me, and I shall give thee . . ." The Father gave the Son the place and the power to act upon Him. The asking of the Son was no mere show or shadow, but one of those life-movements in which the love of the Father and the Son met and completed each other. The Father had determined that He should not be alone in His counsels: there was a Son on whose asking and accepting their fulfillment should depend. So there was in the very being and life of God an asking of which prayer on earth was to be the reflection and the outflow. It was not without including this that Jesus said, "I knew that thou hearest me always." Just as the sonship of Jesus on earth may not be separated from His sonship in heaven, even so His prayer on earth is the continuation and counterpart of His asking in heaven. The prayer of the man Christ Jesus is the link between the eternal asking of the only-begotten Son in the bosom of the Father and the prayer of men upon earth. Prayer has its rise and its deepest source in the very being of God. In the bosom of Deity nothing is ever done without prayer—the asking of the Son and the giving of the Father.[1]

This may help us somewhat to understand how the prayer of man, coming through the Son, can have effect upon God. The decrees of God are not decisions made by Him without reference to the Son, or His petition to be sent up through Him. By no means. The Lord Jesus is the first-begotten, the head and heir of all things: all things were created *through Him* and *unto Him,* and all things consist *in Him.* In the counsels of the Father, the Son, as representative of all creation had always room left for the liberty of the Son as mediator and intercessor, and also for the petitions of all who draw near to the Father in the Son.

If the thought comes that this liberty and power of the Son to act upon the Father is at variance with the immutability of the divine decrees, let us not forget that there is not with God as with man, a past by which He is irrevocably bound. God does not live in time with its past and future. The distinctions of time have no reference to Him who inhabits eternity. Eternity is an ever-present *now*, in which the past is never past and the future always present. To meet our human weakness, Scripture must speak of past decrees and a coming future. In reality, the immutability of God's counsel is still always in perfect harmony with His liberty to do whatsoever He will. The prayers of the Son and His people were not taken up into the eternal decrees so that their effect should only be an apparent one. Instead, the Father-heart holds itself open and free to listen to every prayer that rises through the Son; God does indeed allow himself to be decided by prayer to do what He otherwise would not have done.

This perfect harmony and union of divine sovereignty and human liberty is to us an unfathomable mystery, because God as the *Eternal One* transcends all our thoughts. But let it be our comfort and strength to be assured that in the eternal fellowship of the Father and the Son, the power of prayer has its origin and certainty, and that through our union with the Son, our prayer is taken up and can have its influence in the inner life of the Blessed Trinity.

God's decrees are no iron framework against which man's liberty would vainly seek to struggle. No. God himself is the Living Love, who in His Son as man has entered into the tenderest relation with all that is human. God through the Holy Spirit takes up all that is human into the divine life of love, and keeps himself free to give every human prayer its place in His government of the world.

It is in the dawning light of such thoughts that the doctrine of the Blessed Trinity no longer is an abstract speculation, but the living manifestation of the way in which it is possible for man to be taken up into the fellowship of God, and his prayer to become a real factor in God's rule of this earth. We can, as in the distance, catch glimpses of the light that from the eternal world shines out on words such as these: "Through Him we have access by one Spirit unto the Father."

Everlasting God, the Three-One and Thrice Holy, In deep reverence would I with veiled face worship before the holy mystery of your Divine Being. If it please you, most glorious God, to unveil anything of that mystery, I would bow with fear and trembling, lest I sin against you, as I meditate on your glory.

Father, I thank you that you bear this name not only as the Father of your children here on earth, but as having from eternity subsisted as the Father with your only-begotten Son. I thank you that as Father you can hear our prayer, because you have from eternity given a place in your counsels to the asking of your Son. I thank you that we have seen in Him on earth what the blessed relationship was He had with you in heaven; and how from eternity in all your counsels and decrees, there had been room left for His prayers and their answers. And I thank you above all that through His true human nature on your throne above, and through your Holy Spirit in our human nature here below, a way has been opened up by which every human cry of need can be taken up into and touch the life and love of God, and receive in answer whatsoever it shall ask.

Blessed Jesus, in whom as the Son the path of prayer has been opened up, and who gives us assurance of the answer, we beseech you to teach your people to pray. Each day let this be the sign of our sonship, that, like you, we know that the Father hears us always. Amen.

NOTE

God hears prayer. This simplest view of prayer is taken throughout Scripture. It dwells not on the reflex influence of prayer on our heart and life, although it abundantly shows the connection between prayer as an act, and prayer as a state. It rather fixes with great definiteness the objective or real purposes of prayer: to obtain blessing, gifts, deliverances from God. "Ask and it shall be given," Jesus says.

"However true and valuable the reflection may be, that God, foreseeing and foreordaining all things, has also foreseen and foreordained our prayers as links in the chain of events, of cause and effect, as a real power; yet we feel convinced that this is not the light in which the mind can find peace in this great subject, nor do we think that here is the attractive power to draw us in prayer. We feel rather that such a reflection *diverts* the attention from the Object whence comes the impulse, life, and strength of prayer. The living God, *contemporary and not merely eternal,*[2] the living, merciful, Holy One, God manifesting himself to the soul, God saying, 'Seek my face'; this is the magnet that draws us, this alone can open heart and lips. . . .

"In Jesus Christ the Son of God, we have the full solution of the difficulty. He prayed on earth, and that not merely as man, but as the Son of God incarnate. His prayer on earth is only the manifestation of His prayer from all eternity, when in the divine counsel He was set up as the Christ. . . . The Son was appointed to be heir of all things. From all eternity the Son of God was the way, the mediator. He was, to use our imperfect language, from eternity speaking unto the Father on behalf of the world."— Saphir, *The Hidden Life,* also *The Lord's Prayer.*

---

[1]See this thought developed in R. Löber, *Die Lehre vom Gebet.*

[2]Should it not rather be *contemporary, because eternal,* in the proper meaning of this latter word?

LESSON EIGHTEEN

Prayer in Harmony with the Destiny of Man

"And he saith unto them, Whose is this image and super-scription?" (Matt. 22:20).
"And God said, Let us make man in our image, after our like-ness" (Gen. 1:26).

"Whose is this image?" By this question Jesus foiled His ene-mies when they planned to trick Him, and He settled the matter of duty in regard to the tribute. The question and the principle it involves are of universal application, nowhere more truly than in man himself. The image he bears decides his destiny. Bearing God's image, he belongs to God. Prayer to God is what he was created for. Prayer is part of the wonderful likeness he bears to His divine original; of the deep mystery of the fellowship of love in which the Triune God has His blessedness, prayer is the earth-ly image and likeness.

The more we meditate on what prayer is, and its wonderful power with God, the more we feel constrained to ask, "Who—and what—is man that such a place in God's counsels should have been allotted to him?" Sin has so degraded him that from what he is now, we can form no conception of what he was meant to be.

We must turn back to God's own record of man's creation to discover there what God's purpose was, and what capacities man was endowed with for the fulfillment of that purpose.

Man's destiny appears clearly from God's language at creation. It was to *fill,* to *subdue,* to *have dominion* over the earth and all in it. All the three expressions show us that man was meant, as God's representative, to hold rule here on earth. As God's viceroy, he was to fill God's place. Himself subject to God, he was to keep all else in subjection to Him. It was the will of God that all that was to be done on earth should be done through him. The history of the earth was to be entirely in his hands.

In accordance with such a destiny was the position he was to occupy, and the power at his disposal. When an earthly sovereign sends a representative to a distant province, it is understood that he advises as to the policy to be adopted, and that that advice is acted on. He is at liberty to apply for troops and the other means needed for carrying out the policy or maintaining the dignity of the empire. If his policy be not approved of, he is recalled to make way for someone who better understands his sovereign's desires. As long as he is trusted, his advice is carried out. As God's representative, man was to have ruled. All was to have been done under his will and rule. On his advice and at his request, heaven was to have bestowed its blessing on earth. His prayer was to have been the wonderful, though simple and most natural channel, in which the close relationship between the King in heaven and man, His faithful servant as lord of this world, was to have been maintained. The destinies of the world were given into the power of the wishes, the will, the prayer of man.

With sin, all this underwent a terrible change: man's fall brought all creation under the curse. With redemption the beginning of a glorious restoration was seen. No sooner had God begun in Abraham to form for himself a people from whom kings—even the Great King—should come forth than we see what power the prayer of God's faithful servant has to decide the destinies of those who come into contact with him. In Abraham we see how prayer is not only, or even chiefly, the means of obtaining blessing for ourselves. Rather, it is the exercise of his royal prerogative to influence the destinies of men and the will of God which rules them. Not once do we find Abraham praying for himself. His prayer for Sodom and Lot, for Abimelech, for Ishmael, prove what power a man, who is God's friend, has to make the history of those around him.

This had been man's destiny from the first. Scripture not only tells us this, but also teaches us how it was that God could entrust man with such a high calling. It was because He had created him *in His own image and likeness.* The external rule was not committed to him without the inner fitness. Bearing God's image in having dominion, in being lord of all, had its root in the inner likeness, in his nature. An inner agreement and harmony existed between God and man, an incipient godlikeness, which fitted man to be the mediator between God and His world. Since he was to be prophet, priest, and king he was to interpret God's will, to represent nature's needs, to receive and dispense God's bounty. In bearing God's image, he could bear God's rule. Indeed, he was so like God, so capable of entering into God's purposes and carrying out His plans, that God could trust him with the wonderful privilege of asking and obtaining what the world might need.

Although sin has for a time frustrated God's plans, prayer still remains what it would have been if man had never fallen— the proof of man's godlikeness, his link with the Infinite Unseen One, the power that is allowed to hold the hand that holds the destinies of the universe. Prayer is not merely the cry of the supplicant for mercy; it is the highest expression of His will by man, who knows himself to be of divine origin, created for and capable of being, in king-like liberty, the executor of the counsels of the Eternal.

What sin destroyed, grace has restored. What the first Adam lost, the second has won back. In Christ man regains his original position, and the Church, abiding in Christ, inherits the promise: "Ask what ye will, and it shall be done unto you."

By no means does such a promise refer primarily to the grace or blessing we need for ourselves. It refers to our position as fruit-bearing branches of the Heavenly Vine, who, like Him, live only for the work and glory of the Father. It is for those who abide in Him, who have forsaken self to abide in Him with His life of obedience and self-sacrifice, those who have lost their life and found it in Him, and are now entirely given up to the interests of the Father and His kingdom. These are they who understand how their new creation has brought them back to their original destiny, has restored God's image and likeness, and with it the power to have dominion. Such have indeed the power, each in their own circle, to obtain and dispense the powers of heaven here on earth. With holy boldness they may make known what they will. They live as priests in God's presence. As kings the powers of the world to come begin to be at their disposal.[1] They enter upon the fulfillment of the promise: "Ask what ye will, and it shall be done unto you."

Church of the living God, your calling is higher and holier than you know. Through your members, as kings and priests unto God, would God rule the world; their prayers bestow and withhold the blessings of heaven. His elect are not just content to be themselves saved. Instead, they yield themselves wholly, that through them, just as through the Son, the Father may fulfill all His glorious counsel. In these His elect, who cry day and night unto Him, God would prove how wonderful man's original destiny was.

As the image-bearer of God on earth, the earth was indeed given into man's hand. When he fell, all fell with him; the whole creation groans and travails in pain together. But now he is redeemed, and the restoration of the original dignity has begun. It is God's purpose that the fulfillment of His eternal purpose and the coming of His kingdom should depend on those of His people who, abiding in Christ, are ready to take up their position in Him their head, the great Priest-King, and in their prayers are bold enough to say what they will that their God should do. As image-bearer and representative of God on earth, redeemed man by his prayers determines the history of this earth. Man was created, and has now again been redeemed, to pray and by his prayer to have dominion.

Lord, what is man that you are mindful of him? And the son of man, that you visit him? You have made him a little lower than the angels, and have crowned him with glory and honor.

You made him to have dominion over the work of your hands. You have put all things under his feet. O Lord, our Lord, how excellent is your name in all the earth!

Lord God, how low sin has made man sink. How terribly it has darkened his mind that he does not even know his divine destiny: to be your servant and representative. How sad that even your people, when their eyes are opened, are so slow to accept their calling and seek to have power with God in order to have power with men, too, to bless them.

Lord Jesus, in you the Father has again crowned man with glory and honor, and opened the way for us to be what he would have us to be. O Lord, have mercy on your people, and visit your heritage! Work mightily in your Church, and teach your believing disciples to go forth in their royal priesthood and in the power of prayer, to which you have given such wonderful promises. Teach them to serve your kingdom, to have rule over the nations and make the name of God glorious in the earth. Amen.

---

[1]God is seeking priests among the sons of men. A human priesthood is one of the essential parts of His eternal plan. To *rule* creation by man is His design; to carry on the worship of creation by man is no less part of His design.

Priesthood is the appointed link between heaven and earth, the channel of intercourse between the sinner and God. Such a priesthood, insofar as expiation is concerned, is in the hands of the Son of God alone; insofar as it is to be the medium of communication between Creator and creature, is also in the hands of redeemed men—of the Church of God.

God is seeking kings, not out of the ranks of angels. Fallen man must furnish Him with the rulers of His universe. Human hands must wield the sceptre, human heads must wear the crown.—*The Rent Veil,* by Dr. H. Bonar.

Power for Praying and Working

"Verily, verily, I say unto you, He that believeth on me, the works that I do shall he do also; and *greater works* than these shall he do; because I go unto my Father. *And whatsoever ye shall ask* in my name, that will I do . . ." (John 14:12, 13).

The Saviour opened His public ministry with His disciples by the Sermon on the Mount. Now He closes it by the parting address preserved for us by John. In both He speaks more than once of prayer—but with a difference. The Sermon on the Mount is to disciples who have just entered His school, who scarcely know that God is their Father, and whose prayer chiefly has reference to their personal needs. In His closing address, He speaks to disciples whose training time has now come to an end, and who are ready as His messengers to take His place and do His works. In the former, the chief lesson is: Be childlike, pray believingly, and trust the Father to give you all good gifts. Now He points to something higher. They are now His friends to whom He has made known all that He has heard of the Father. They are His messengers, who have entered into His plans and into whose hands the care of His work and kingdom on earth is to be entrusted. They are to go out and do His works, and, in the power of His approaching exaltation, even greater works. Prayer is to be the channel through which that power is to be received for their work. With Christ's ascension to the Father, a new epoch begins, both for their working and praying.

How clearly this connection comes out in our text. As Christ's body here on earth, as those who are one with Him in heaven, the disciples are now to do greater works than He had done. Their success and their victories are to be greater than His. He mentions two reasons for this: one, because He was to go to the Father, to receive all power; the other, because they might now ask and expect all in His name. "Because I go to the Father, *and* [notice this and] whatever ye shall ask I will do." His going to the Father would in this way bring a double blessing. They would ask and receive all in His name, and as a consequence, would do the greater works. The first mention of prayer in our Saviour's parting words thus teaches us two most important lessons. He that would do the works of Jesus *must pray* in His name. He that would pray in His name *must work* in His name.

He who would work *must pray*. In prayer, power for work is obtained. He that in faith would do the works that Jesus did must pray in His name. As long as Jesus was here on earth, He himself did the greatest works. Devils the disciples could not cast out fled at His word. When Jesus went to the Father, He was no longer here in the body to work directly. Now the disciples were His body. All His work from the throne in heaven here on earth must and could be done through them.

One might have thought that since He was leaving the scene himself, and could only work through commissioners, the works might now be fewer and weaker. He assures us of the contrary: "*Verily, verily,* I say unto you, He that believeth on me, the works that I do shall he do also; and greater works than these shall he do." His approaching death was to break down and make an end of the power of sin. With the resurrection the powers of the Eternal Life were truly to take possession of the human body and to obtain supremacy over human life. With His ascension He was to receive the power to communicate the Holy Spirit to His own. The union, the oneness between himself on the throne and them on earth, was to be so intensely and divinely perfect that He meant it as literal truth: "Greater works than these shall he do, because I go to the Father." And the results proved how true it was.

Jesus, during three years of personal labor on earth, gathered little more than five hundred disciples, and most of them so feeble that they were but little credit to His cause. Men like Peter and Paul manifestly were allowed to do greater things than He had done. From the throne Jesus could do through them what He himself in His humiliation could not yet do.

But there is one condition: "He that believeth on me . . . shall . . . do greater works, because I go unto my Father. *And whatsoever ye shall ask in my name, that will I do.*" His going to the Father would give Him new power to hear prayer. Two things were needed for doing the greater works: His going to the Father to receive all power and our prayer in His name to receive all power from Him again. As He asks the Father, He receives and bestows on us the power of the new dispensation for the greater works. As we believe, and ask in His name, the power comes and takes possession of us to do the greater works.

How much striving there is in the work of God, in which there is little or nothing to be seen of the power to do anything like Christ's works, not to speak of greater works. There can be but one reason: believing on Him, the believing prayer in His name, is missing.

How good if every laborer and leader in church, or school, in the work of home or foreign missions, would learn the lesson: Prayer in the name of Jesus is the way to share in the mighty power which Jesus has received of the Father for His people. In this power alone he that believes can do the greater works. To every complaint about weakness or unfitness, as to difficulties or lack of success, Jesus gives this one answer: "*He that believeth on me . . . shall do . . . greater works; because I go to the Father. And whatsoever ye shall ask* in my name, *that will I do.*" We must understand that the most important thing for everyone who would do the work of Jesus is to believe, and so get linked to Him, the Almighty One, and then to pray the prayer of faith in His name. Without this our work is only human and carnal. It may help in restraining sin or preparing the way for blessing, but the real power is wanting. Effective working first needs effective prayer.

The second lesson is: He who would pray *must work*. It is for power to work that prayer has such great promises. In working, power for the effective prayer of faith will be gained.

In these parting words of our Lord no less than six times (John 14:13, 14; 15:7, 16; 16:23, 24) He repeats those unlimited prayer-promises which have so often awakened our anxious questionings as to their real meaning: *whatsoever, anything, what ye will, ask and ye shall receive*. How many a believer has read these over with joy and hope, and in deep earnestness of soul has sought to plead them for his own need—only to come out disappointed. The simple reason was that he separated the promise from its surroundings. The Lord gave the wonderful promise of the free use of His name with the Father in connection with *doing His works*. It is the disciple who gives himself wholly to live for Jesus' work and kingdom, for His will and honor, to whom the power will come to appropriate the promise. He who tries to grasp the promise when he wants something very special for himself will be disappointed, because he is trying to make Jesus the servant of his own comfort. But one who seeks to pray the effective prayer of faith because he needs it for the work of the Master, he will learn it—because he has made himself the servant of his Lord's interests. Prayer not only teaches and strengthens to work: work teaches and strengthens to pray.

This is in perfect harmony with a truth in both the natural and the spiritual world. Whosoever hath, to him shall be given; or, he that is faithful in a little, is faithful also in much. With the small measure of grace already received, we should give ourselves to the Master for His work. Work will be to us a real school of prayer. When Moses had to take full charge of a rebellious people, he felt the need—but also the courage—to speak boldly to God and to ask great things of Him (Ex. 33:12, 15, 18). As you give yourself entirely to God for His work, you will feel that nothing less than these great promises are what you need and that nothing less is what you may most confidently expect.

Believer in Jesus, you are called and appointed to do the works of Jesus, and even greater works, because He has gone to the Father to receive the power to do them in and through you. "*Whatsoever* ye shall ask in my name, that *will I do.*" Give yourself, and live, to do the works of Christ, and then you will learn to pray so that you obtain wonderful answers to prayer. Give yourself, and live, to pray and you will learn to do the works He did—and greater works. With disciples full of faith in Him and bold in prayer to ask great things, Christ can conquer the world.

My Lord, again this day I have heard words from you which pass my comprehension. And yet I can do nothing except in simple, childlike faith take and keep them as your gift to me too. You have said that because of your going to the Father, he that believes on you will do the works which you have done, and greater works. Lord, I worship you as the Glorified One, and look for the fulfillment of your promise. May my whole life just be one of continued believing in you. Purify and sanctify my heart and make it so tenderly susceptible to you and your love, so that believing on you may be the very life it breathes.

You have said because of your going to the Father, you will do whatsoever we ask. From your throne of power you would make your people share the power given to you, and work through them as the members of your body, in response to their believing prayers in your Name. Power in prayer with you, and power in work with men, is what you have promised your people—and me too.

Blessed Lord, forgive us that we have so little believed you and your promise, and have so seldom proved your faithfulness in fulfilling it. Forgive us that we have so little honored your all-prevailing name in heaven or upon the earth.

Lord, teach me to pray so that I may prove that your name is indeed all-prevailing with God and men and devils. Teach me so to work and so to pray that you can glorify yourself in me as the Omnipotent One, and do your great works through me too. Amen.

The Chief End of Prayer

"I go unto my Father. And whatsoever ye shall ask in my name, that will I do, that the Father may be glorified in the Son" (John 14:12, 13).

That the Father may be glorified in the Son. For this reason Jesus on His throne in glory will do all we ask in His name. Every answer to prayer He gives will have this as its object: when there is no prospect of the Father being glorified, He will not answer. So, with us as with Jesus, the essential element in our petitions must be that the glory of the Father be the aim and end, the very soul and life of our prayer.

It was so with Jesus when He was on earth. "I seek not mine own honor: I seek the honor of him that sent me"; in these words we have the keynote of His life. In the first words of the high-priestly prayer He expresses it: "Father! glorify thy Son, *that thy Son may glorify thee.*" "*I have glorified thee* on earth; glorify me with thyself." The ground on which He asks to be taken up into the glory He had with the Father is twofold: He has glorified Him on earth; He will still glorify Him in heaven. What He asks is only to enable Him to glorify the Father more. As we agree with Jesus on this point, and please Him by making the Father's glory our chief object in prayer too, our prayer cannot fail to be answered.

Jesus said distinctly that nothing glorifies the Father more than His doing what we ask. He will not, therefore, let any opportunity slip of answering these prayers. Let us make His aim ours. Let the glory of the Father be the link between our asking and His doing. Prayer like that must prevail.[1]

This word of Jesus comes indeed as a sharp two-edged sword, piercing even to the dividing of soul and spirit, and quick to discern the thoughts and intents of the heart. Jesus in His prayers on earth, in His intercession in heaven, in His promise of an answer to our prayers from there, makes this His first object—the glory of His Father. Is it so with us too? Or are self-interest and self-will the strongest motives urging us to pray? Or, if not, do we have to confess that the distinct, conscious longing for the glory of the Father is not what animates our prayers? And yet it must be so.

Not that the believer does not at times want to pray with that motive. But he grieves that he seldom does so. He knows the reason for his failure too. The separation between the spirit of daily life and the spirit of the hour of prayer was too wide. We begin to see that the desire for the glory of the Father is not something that we can arouse and present to our Lord only when we prepare ourselves to pray. No! Only when the whole life, in all its parts, is surrendered to God's glory can we really pray to His glory too. "*Do all* to the glory of God," and "*Ask all* to the glory of God"— these twin commands are inseparable. Obedience to the former is the secret of grace for the latter. A life yielded to the glory of God is the condition for the prayers that Jesus can answer, "that the Father may be glorified."

This demand in connection with prevailing prayer—that it should be to the glory of God—is no more than right and natural. There is none glorious but the Lord; there is no glory except His and what He gives to His creatures. Creation exists to show forth His glory. All that is not for His glory is sin and darkness and death. Only in the glorifying of God can the creatures find glory. What the Son of Man did—to give himself wholly, His whole life, to glorify the Father—is nothing but the simple duty of every redeemed one. He will share Christ's reward too. Because Christ gave himself so entirely to the glory of the Father, the Father crowned him with glory and honor, giving the kingdom into His hands, with power to ask what He will, and as Intercessor to answer our prayers. And just as we become one with Christ in this, and as our prayer is part of a life utterly surrendered to God's glory, so will the Saviour be able to glorify the Father to us by the fulfillment of the promise: "Whatsoever ye shall ask, *I will do it.*"

Such a life, with God's glory our only aim, we cannot attain by any effort of our own. Only in the man Christ Jesus is such a life to be seen, but in Him it is also possible for us. Yes, blessed be God! His life is our life. He gave *himself* for us; He himself is now our life.

The discovery of self as usurping the place of God and the confession and the denial of self-seeking and self-trusting, is essential—but that is what we cannot accomplish in our own strength. Only Jesus himself can cast out all self-glorifying life and give us instead His own God-glorifying life and Spirit. As His presence comes in to dwell and reign in our hearts—this Jesus who longs to glorify the Father in hearing our prayers—He will teach us to live and to pray to the glory of God.

What motive, what power is there that can urge our slothful hearts to yield themselves to our Lord to work this in us? Surely nothing more is needed than a sight of how glorious, how singularly worthy of glory the Father is. Let our faith learn to bow before Him in adoring worship and ascribe to Him alone the kingdom, the power, and the glory. May we yield ourselves to dwell in His light as the ever-blessed, ever-loving One. Surely we shall be stirred to say, "To Him alone be glory." Then we shall look to our Lord Jesus with new intensity of desire for a life that refuses to see or seek anything other than the glory of God.

When there is but little prayer that can be answered, the Father is not glorified. It is a duty to live and pray so that our prayer can be answered and glorify God. For the sake of God's glory, let us learn to pray well.

How humbling that so often there is earnest prayer for someone or something in which the thought of our joy or our pleasure was far stronger than any yearning for God's glory. No wonder that there are so many unanswered prayers. Here we see the secret. God would not be glorified when His glory was not our object. He who wants to pray the prayer of faith will have to live literally so that the Father may be glorified in him in all things. This must be his aim. Without this there cannot be the prayer of faith.

"How can ye believe," said Jesus, "which receive glory of one another, and the glory that cometh from the only God ye seek not?" All seeking of our own glory with men makes faith impossible. The deep, intense self-sacrifice that gives up its own glory and seeks the glory of God alone, that wakens in the soul that spiritual susceptibility of the divine—that is faith. The surrender to God to seek His glory, and the expectation that He will show His glory in hearing us, are one at root. He that seeks God's glory will see it in the answer to prayer, and he alone.

But how shall we attain to it? Let us begin with confession. How little has the glory of God been an all-absorbing passion. How little have our lives and our prayers been filled with it. How little have we lived in the likeness of the Son and in sympathy with Him—for God and His glory alone. Let us take time until the Holy Spirit reveals it to us, and we see how we have sinned in this. True knowledge and confession of sin are the sure path to deliverance.

Looking to Jesus, we can see by what death we can glorify God. In death He glorified Him. Through death He was glorified with Him. By dying, being dead to self and living to God, we can glorify Him. This death to self, this life to the glory of God, is what Jesus gives and lives in each one who can trust Him for it. Let nothing less than these—the desire and decision to live only for the glory of the Father as Christ did; the acceptance of Him with His life and strength working it in us; the joyful assurance that we can live to the glory of God because Christ lives is us—let this be the spirit of our daily life. Jesus stands surety for our living in this way. The Holy Spirit is given, and waiting to make it our experience, if we will only trust and let Him. Let us not hold back through unbelief, but confidently take as our watchword: *all* to the glory of God! The Father accepts the will and the sacrifice is pleasing to Him. Then the Holy Spirit will seal us within with the consciousness that we are living for God and His glory.

What quiet peace and power there will be in our prayers, when we know ourselves, through His grace to be in perfect harmony with Him who promises to do what we ask: "That the Father may be glorified in the Son." With our whole being consciously yielded to the inspiration of the Word and Spirit, our desires will be no longer ours but His, with their chief end the glory of God. With increasing liberty we shall be able to pray: "Father, you know that we ask it only for your glory."

The condition of prayer answers, instead of being like a mountain we cannot climb, will give us the greater confidence that we shall be heard, because we have seen that prayer has no higher beauty or blessedness than this, that it glorifies the Father. And the precious privilege of prayer will become doubly precious because it brings us into perfect unison with the Beloved Son in the wonderful partnership He proposes: "*You ask*, and *I do*, that the Father may be glorified in the Son."

Blessed Lord Jesus, I come again to you. Every lesson you give me convinces me more deeply how little I know to pray in the right way. But every lesson also inspires me with hope that you are going to teach me and that you are teaching me not only what prayer should be, but how to pray as I ought. Lord, I look with courage to you—the great Intercessor, who prays and hears prayer—only for the Father to be glorified. Teach me also to live and to pray to the glory of God.

To this end I yield myself to you again. I would be nothing. I have given self to death as already crucified with you. Through the Spirit, self's workings are mortified and dead. Your life and your love of the Father are taking possession of me. A new longing begins to fill my soul, that every day, every hour, in every prayer the glory of the Father may be everything to me. Lord, I am in your school to learn this. Teach me.

God of glory, the Father of glory, my God and my Father, accept the desire of a child who has seen that your glory alone is worth living for. Lord, show me your glory. Let it overshadow me. Let it fill the temple of my heart. Let me dwell in it as revealed in Christ. Fulfill in me your own good pleasure, that your child should find his glory in seeking the glory of his Father. Amen.

---

[1]See in the note on George Muller, at the close of this volume, how he was led to make God's *glory* his first object.

LESSON TWENTY-ONE

The All-Inclusive Condition

"If ye abide in me, and my words abide in you, ask whatsoever
ye will, and it shall be done unto you" (John 15:7, ASV).

In all God's dealings with us, the promise and its conditions
are inseparable. If we fulfill the conditions, He fulfills the promise. What He is to be to us depends upon what we are willing to
be to Him. "Draw near to God, and he will draw near to you."
And so in prayer the unlimited promise, *ask whatsoever ye will,*
has one simple and natural condition, *if ye abide in me.* It is
Christ whom the Father always hears. God is *in Christ,* and can
be reached only by being in Him. To be *in Him* is the way to have
our prayer heard. Fully and wholly *abiding in Him,* we have the
right to ask whatsoever we will, and the promise that it shall be
done unto us.

When we compare this promise with the experience of most
believers, we are startled by a terrible discrepancy. Who could
count the countless prayers that rise and bring no answer? Why?
Either we do not fulfill the condition or God does not fulfill the
promise.

Believers are not willing to admit either, and therefore have
devised a way of escape from the dilemma. They add to the
promise the qualifying clause our Saviour did not put there: if it

120

be God's will. That way they maintain both God's integrity and their own. How sad that they do not accept and hold it fast as it stands, trusting Christ to vindicate His truth. Then God's Spirit would lead them to see the divine propriety of such a promise to those who really abide in Christ in the sense in which He means it, and to confess that the failure in fulfilling the condition is the one sufficient explanation of unanswered prayer. How the Holy Spirit would then make the feebleness in prayer one of the mightiest motives to urge us on to discover the secret, and obtain the blessing, of full abiding in Christ.

"If ye abide in me." As a Christian grows in grace and in the knowledge of the Lord Jesus, he is often surprised to find how the words of God grow in new and deeper meaning. He can look back to the day when some word of God was opened up to him and the blessing he had found in it. After a time some deeper experience gave it a new meaning, and it was as if he never had seen what it contained. Again, later, as he advanced in the Christian life, the same word came to him as a great mystery, until the Holy Spirit led him still deeper into its divine fullness. One of these ever-growing, never-exhausted words that open up to us step by step the fullness of the divine life is the Master's precious "abide in me." As the union of the branch with the vine is one of unceasing growth and increase, so our abiding in Christ is a life process in which the divine life takes ever fuller and more complete possession of us. The young and feeble believer may be really abiding in Christ up to the measure of his light; he who reaches onward to the full abiding in the sense in which the Master understood the words is he who inherits all the promises connected with it.

In the growing life of abiding in Christ, the first stage is that of faith. The believer sees that, in spite of all his feebleness, the command is really meant for him. Then his aim is simply to believe that, just as he knows he is in Christ, so in spite of unfaithfulness and failure, abiding in Christ is his immediate duty and a blessing within his reach. He is especially occupied with the love, and power, and faithfulness of the Saviour. He feels his one need is to believe.

Before long he sees something more is needed. Obedience and faith must go together. Not as if obedience must be added to the faith he has, but faith must be made manifest in obedience. Faith is obedience at home and looking to the Master; obedience is faith going out to do His will. He sees how he has been more occupied with the privilege and the blessings of this abiding than with its duties and its fruit. There has been much of self and of self-will that has been unnoticed or tolerated. The peace which, as a young and feeble disciple, he could enjoy in believing, goes from him. It is in practical obedience that the abiding must be maintained: "If ye keep my commands, ye shall abide in my love." Before his great aim was to let the heart rest on Christ and His promises through the *mind*, and the truth it took hold of. Now, in this stage, his chief effort is to get his *will* united with the will of his Lord, and the heart and the life brought entirely under His rule.

But it seems as if there is something missing. The will and the heart are on Christ's side. He obeys and he loves his Lord. But why is it that the fleshly nature still has so much power? Or why are the spontaneous motions and emotions of the inmost being not what they should be? The will does not approve or allow, but here is a region beyond control of the will. Why also—even when there is not so much of positive commission to condemn—is there so much omission, so much deficiency of that beauty of holiness? Where is that zeal of love, that conformity to Jesus and His death in which the life of self is lost, and which is surely implied in the abiding, as the Master described it? There must surely be something in our abiding in Christ and Christ in us, which a young Christian has not yet experienced.

That is true. Faith and obedience are only the pathway of blessing. Before giving us the parable of the vine and the branches, Jesus very distinctly told what the full blessing is toward which faith and obedience should lead. Three times He said, "If ye love me, keep my commandments," and spoke of the threefold blessing with which He would crown such obedient love. The Holy Spirit would come from the Father; the Son would manifest himself; the Father and the Son would come and make their abode.

As our faith grows into obedience, our whole being goes out and clings to Christ in obedience and love. Then our inner life opens up, and the capacity is formed within to receive the life and spirit of the glorified Jesus, as a distinct and conscious union with Christ and with the Father. The word is fulfilled in us: "In that day ye shall know that I am in my Father and ye in me, and I in you."

We see that, just as Christ is in God and God in Christ, not only one in will and in love, but also in identity of nature and life because they exist in each other, so we are in Christ and Christ in us, a union not only of will and love but of life and nature too.

After Jesus had spoken of our knowing through the Holy Spirit that He is in the Father, and we in Him and He in us, He said, "Abide in me, and I in you. Accept, consent to receive that divine life of union with me, in virtue of which, as you abide in me, I also abide in you, even as I abide in the Father. So that your life is mine and mine is yours."

This is abiding and occupying the position in which Christ can come and abide; truly abiding in Him so that the soul has drawn away from self and finds that He has taken that place of self and become our life. It is becoming like little children who have no care, and find their happiness in trusting and obeying the love that has done all for them.

To those who abide like this, the promise comes as their rightful heritage: Ask whatsoever ye will. It cannot be otherwise. Christ has full possession of them. Christ dwells in their love, their will, their life. Not only has their will been given up, but Christ has entered it. There He dwells and breathes into it His Spirit. He whom the Father always hears, prays in them. They pray in Him. What they ask shall be done for them.

Fellow believer, let us confess that it is because we do not abide in Christ as he would have us abide, that the Church is so impotent in the presence of infidelity and worldliness and heathendom, in the midst of which the Lord is able to make her more than conqueror. Let us believe that He means what He promises, and accept the condemnation the confession implies.

But let us not be discouraged. The abiding of the branch in the Vine is a life of never-ceasing growth. The abiding as the Master meant it is within our reach, for He lives to give it to us. Only let us be ready to count all things loss and say, "Not as though I had already attained; I follow after, if that I may apprehend that for which I also am apprehended of Christ Jesus." Let us not be so much occupied with the abiding as with *Him* to whom the abiding links us and His fullness. Let it be *Him*, the whole Christ, in His obedience and humiliation, in His exaltation and power, in whom our soul moves and acts. He himself will fulfill His promise in us.

As we abide and continue to grow into the full abiding, let us exercise our right—the will to enter into all God's will. Obeying what that will commands, let us claim what it promises. Let us yield to the teaching of the Holy Spirit, who shows each of us, according to his growth and measure, what we may claim in prayer as God's will for us. Let us rest content with nothing less than the personal experience of what Jesus gave when He said, "If ye abide in me, ask whatsoever ye will, it shall be done unto you."

Beloved Lord, teach me to take this promise anew in all its simplicity, and to be sure that the only measure of your holy giving is our holy willing. Lord, let each word of this promise be made vital and powerful in my soul.

You say: Abide in me! Master, my life and my all, I do abide in you. Help me to grow up into all your fullness. It is not the effort of faith, seeking to cling to you, nor even the rest of faith, trusting you to keep me; it is not the obedience of the will, nor the keeping the commandments that can satisfy me. Only you yourself living in me just as in the Father will satisfy. It is you, my Lord, no longer before me and above me, but one with me, and abiding in me; it is this I need, it is this I seek. It is this I trust you for.

You say: Ask whatsoever ye will! Lord, I know that the life of full, deep abiding will so renew and sanctify and strengthen the will that I shall have the light and the liberty to ask great things. Lord, let my will, dead in your death, living in your life, be bold and large in its petitions.

You say: It shall be done. You who are the Amen, the Faithful and True Witness, give me in yourself the joyous confidence that you will make this word yet more wonderfully true to me than ever, because "it hath not entered into the heart of man to

conceive what God hath prepared for them that love Him."
Amen.

NOTE

On a thoughtful comparison of what we mostly find in books
or sermons on prayer, and the teaching of the Master, we shall
find one great difference: the importance assigned to the answer
to prayer is by no means the same. In the former we find a great
deal on the blessing of prayer as a spiritual exercise even if there
be no answer, and on the reasons why we should be content without it. God's fellowship ought to be more to us than the gift we
ask; God's wisdom only knows what is best; God may bestow
something better than what He withholds. Though this teaching
looks very high and spiritual, it is remarkable that we find nothing of it with our Lord. The more carefully we gather together all
He spoke on prayer, the clearer it becomes that He wished us to
think of prayer simply as the means to an end, and that the answer was to be the proof that we and our prayer are acceptable to
the Father in heaven. It is not that Christ would have us count
the gifts of higher value than the fellowship and favor of the
Father. By no means. But the Father means the answer to be the
token of his favor and of the reality of our fellowship with Him.
"Today thy servant knoweth that I have found grace in thy sight,
my lord, O king, in that the king hath fulfilled the request of his
servant."

A life marked by daily answer to prayer is the proof of our
spiritual maturity: that we have indeed attained to the true
abiding in Christ; that our will is truly at one with God's will;
that our faith has grown strong to see and take what God has prepared for us; that the name of Christ and His nature have taken
full possession of us; and that we have been found fit to take a
place among those whom God admits to His counsels, and according to whose prayer He rules the world. These are they in
whom something of man's original dignity has been restored, in
whom, as they abide in Christ, His power as the all-prevailing Intercessor can manifest itself, in whom the glory of His name is
shown forth. Prayer is very blessed; *the answer is more blessed*

still, as the response from the Father that our prayer, our faith, our will are indeed as He would wish them to be.

I say these things to encourage you to put together all Christ's teaching about prayer and to believe the truth that when prayer is what it should be, or rather when we are what we should be— abiding in Christ—the answer must be expected. It will bring us out from those refuges where we have comforted ourselves with unanswered prayer. It will show us the place of power to which Christ has appointed His Church, and which it so little occupies. It will reveal the terrible feebleness of our spiritual life as the cause of our not praying boldly in Christ's name. It will urge us mightily to rise to a life of full union with Christ and fullness of the Spirit as the secret of effective prayer. It will lead us on to realize our destiny: *"At that day:* Verily, verily, I say unto you, If ye shall ask anything of the Father, he will give it to you in my name: ask, and ye shall receive, that your joy may be fulfilled." Prayer that is spiritually *in union with Jesus* is always answered.

LESSON TWENTY-TWO

The Word and Prayer

"If ye abide in me, *and my words abide in you,* ask whatsoever ye will, and it shall be done unto you" (John 15:7, ASV).

The vital connection between the word and prayer is one of the simplest and earliest lessons of the Christian life. As one newly converted pagan put it: I pray—I speak to my Father; I read—my Father speaks to me. Before prayer, it is God's Word that prepares me for it, by revealing what the Father has told me to ask. In prayer, it is God's Word that strengthens me by giving my faith its grounds for asking. And after prayer, it is God's Word that brings me the answer, for through that the Spirit shows me I have heard the Father's voice. Prayer is not monologue but dialogue; God's voice in response to mine is its most essential part. Listening to God's voice is the secret of the assurance that He will listen to mine. "Incline thine ear, and hear"; "Give ear to me"; "Hearken to my voice"; are words which God speaks to man as well as man to God. His hearkening will depend on ours. The entrance His words find with me will be the measure of the power of my words with Him. What God's words are to me is the test of what He himself is to me, and so of the uprightness of my desire after Him in prayer.

127

Jesus points to this connection between His Word and our prayer when He says, "If ye abide in me, *and my words abide in you,* ask whatsoever ye will, and it shall be done unto you." The deep importance of this truth becomes clear if we notice the other expression of which this one has taken the place. More than once Jesus had said, "Abide in me and *I in you.*" His abiding in us was the complement and the crown of our abiding in Him. But here, instead of "Ye in me *and I in you,*" He says, "Ye in me *and my words in you.*" His words abiding are the equivalent of himself abiding.

What a view is here opened up to us of the place the words of God in Christ are to have in our spiritual life, especially in our prayer. In a man's words *he reveals himself.* In his promises *he gives himself away,* he binds himself to the one who receives his promise. In his commands he sets forth his will, seeks *to make himself master* of him whose obedience he claims, to guide and use him as if he were part of himself. It is through our words that spirit holds fellowship with spirit, that the spirit of one man passes over and transfers itself into another. It is through the words of a man, heard and accepted, and held fast and obeyed, that he can impart himself to another. But all this in a very relative and limited sense.

But when God, the infinite Being, in whom everything is life and power, spirit and truth, in the very deepest meaning of the words—when God speaks forth himself in His words, He does indeed give himself, His love and His life, His will and His power, to those who receive these words, in a reality passing comprehension. In every promise He puts *himself* in our power to lay hold of and possess; in every command He puts *himself* in our power for us to share with Him His will, His holiness, His perfection. In God's Word God gives us himself. His Word is nothing less than the Eternal Son, Christ Jesus. And so all Christ's words are God's words, full of divine quickening life and power. "The words that I speak unto you, they are spirit and they are life."

Those who study the deaf and dumb tell us how much the power of speaking depends on that of hearing, and how the loss of hearing in children is followed by loss of speaking too. This is true in a wider sense: as we hear, so we speak. This is true in the highest sense of our communion with God. To pray—give utterance to certain wishes and appeal to certain promises—is an easy thing, and can be learned by man through human wisdom. But to pray in the Spirit and speak words that reach and touch God, that affect and influence the powers of the unseen world—such praying, such speaking, depend entirely upon our hearing God's voice. Just as far as we listen to the voice and language that God speaks, and in God's words receive His thoughts, His mind, His life, into our heart, we shall learn to speak in the voice and the language that God hears. It is the ear of the learner, wakened morning by morning, that prepares for the tongue of the learned to speak to God as well as men, as should be (Isa. 50:4).

Hearing the voice of God is something more than the thoughtful study of the Word. There may be a study and knowledge of the Word in which there is but little real fellowship with the living God. But there is also a reading of the Word, in the very presence of the Father and under the leading of the Spirit, in which the Word comes to us in living power from God himself. It is to us the very voice of the Father, a real personal fellowship with himself. It is the living voice of God entering the heart that brings blessing and strength, and awakens the response of a living faith that reaches the heart of God again.

It is on hearing this voice that the power both to obey and believe depends. The chief thing is—not to know *what* God has said we must do but—that *God himself* says it to us. It is not the law, and not the book, not the knowledge of what is right that works obedience, but the personal influence of God and His living fellowship. Even so, it is not the knowledge of *what* God has promised, but the presence of *God himself* as the promiser that awakens faith and trust in prayer. It is only in the full presence of God that disobedience and unbelief become impossible.

"If ye abide in me, and *my words abide in you,* ask whatsoever ye will, and it shall be done unto you." We see what this means. In the words the Saviour gives himself. We must have the words *in us* accepted into our will and life, reproduced in our disposition and conduct. We must have them *abiding* in us—our whole life one continued exposition of the words that are within and filling us; the words revealing Christ within and our life revealing Him without. As the words of Christ enter our very heart, become our life and influence it, our words will enter His heart and influence Him. My prayer will depend on my life. What God's words are to me and in me, my words will be to God and in God. If I do what God says, God will do what I say.

How well the Old Testament saints understood this connection between God's words and ours, and how truly prayer with them was the loving response to what they had heard God speak! If the word were a promise, they counted *on God to do as He had spoken.* "Do as thou hast said"; "For thou, Lord hast spoken it"; "According to thy promise"; "According to thy word." In such expressions they showed that what God promised was the root and the life of what they spoke in prayer. If the word was a command, they simply *did as the Lord had spoken:* "So Abram departed as the Lord had spoken." Their life was fellowship with God in an interchange of word and thought. What God spoke, they heard and did. What they spoke, God heard and did. In each word He speaks to us, the whole Christ gives himself to fulfill it for us. For each word He asks no less than that we give the whole man to keep that word, and to receive its fulfillment.

"If my words abide in you" is a simple and clear condition. In His words His will is revealed. As the words abide in me, His will rules me. My will becomes the empty vessel which His will fills, the willing instrument which His will wields. He fills my inner being. In the exercise of obedience and faith my will becomes ever stronger and is brought into deeper inner harmony with Him. He can fully trust it to will nothing but what He wills. He is not afraid to give the promise, "If my words abide in you, ask whatsoever ye will, and it shall be done unto you." To all who believe and act upon this promise, He will make it literally true.

Disciples of Christ, is it not more and more clear to us that while we have been excusing our unanswered prayers and our impotence in prayer with an imagined submission to God's wisdom and will, the real reason is that our own feeble life is the cause of our feeble prayers?

Nothing but the word coming to us from God's mouth can make strong men. By that we must live. The word of Christ— loved, lived in, abiding in us, becoming through obedience and action part of our being—makes us one with Christ and fits us spiritually for touching, for taking hold of God. All that is of the world passes away; he that does the will of God abides forever. Let us yield heart and life to the words of Christ, the words in which He ever gives himself, the personal living Saviour. Then His promises will be our rich experience: "If ye abide in me, and my words abide in you, ask whatsoever ye will, and it shall be done unto you."

Blessed Lord, today you again revealed my foolishness to me. I see why my prayer has not been more believing and prevailing. I was more occupied with my speaking to you than your speaking to me. I did not understand that the secret of faith is this: there can be only as much faith as there is of the living Word dwelling in the soul.

Your word taught me so clearly: Let every man be swift to hear, slow to speak; let not thine heart be hasty to utter anything before God. Lord, teach me that it is only when your word is accepted into my life that my words can be taken into your heart; that your word, if it be a living power within me, will be a living power with you; what your mouth has spoken, your hands will perform.

Lord, deliver me from the uncircumcised ear. Give me the opened ear of the learner, awakened morning by morning to hear the Father's voice. Even as you speak only what you hear, may my speaking be the echo of your speaking to me. "When Moses went into the tabernacle to speak with him, he heard the voice of One speaking unto him from off the mercy-seat." Lord, may it be so with me too. Let a life and character bearing the one mark— that your words abide and are seen in it—be the preparation for the full blessing: "Ask whatsoever ye will, and it shall be done unto you." Amen.

LESSON TWENTY-THREE

Obedience the Path to Power in Prayer

"Ye have not chosen me, but I have chosen you, and ordained you, that ye should go and bring forth fruit, and that your fruit should remain: that whatsoever ye shall ask of the Father in my name, he may give it to you" (John 15:16).

"The effectual fervent prayer of a *righteous* man availeth much" (James 5:16).

The promise of the Father's giving whatsoever we ask is renewed again in a connection that shows us to whom it is that such wonderful influence in the council chamber of the Most High is to be granted. "I chose you," the Master says, "and appointed you that ye should go and bear fruit, and that your fruit should abide." Then He adds, *to the end* that "whatsoever ye [the fruit-bearing ones] shall ask of the Father in my name, he may give it to you." This is only a fuller expression of what He said, "If ye abide in me." He described the object of this abiding as bearing "fruit," "more fruit," "much fruit": in this was God to be glorified, and the mark of discipleship seen. No wonder that He now adds, that where the reality of the abiding is seen in fruit abounding and abiding, this would be the qualification for praying so as to obtain what we ask. Entire consecration to the fulfillment of our calling is the condition of effective prayer, and the

132

key to the unlimited blessings of Christ's wonderful prayer promises.

Some Christians fear that such a statement is at variance with the doctrine of free grace. But surely not of free grace rightly understood, nor with so many express statements of God's blessed Word. Take the words in 1 John 3:22: "Let us love in deed and truth; *hereby* shall we assure our heart before him. And whatsoever we ask, we receive of him, *because* we keep his commandments, and do the things that are pleasing in his sight." Or take the oft-quoted words of James: "The effectual fervent prayer of a *righteous* man availeth much"; that is, of a man of whom, according to the definition of the Holy Spirit, it can be said, "He that doeth righteousness, is righteous even as he is righteous."

Mark the spirit of so many of the psalms, with their confident appeal to the integrity and righteousness of the supplicant. In Ps. 18:18 David says: "The Lord rewarded me according to my righteousness; according to the cleanness of my hands hath he recompensed me . . . I was also upright before him, and I kept myself from mine iniquity: therefore hath the Lord recompensed me according to my righteousness" (Ps. 18:20, 23, 24). (See also Ps. 7:3-5; 15:1, 2; 17:3, 6; 26:1-6; 119: 121, 153.) If we carefully consider such utterances in the light of the New Testament, we shall find them in perfect harmony with the explicit teaching of the Saviour's parting words: "*if ye keep* my commandments, ye shall abide in my love"; "Ye are my friends *if ye do* what I command you." The word is indeed meant literally: "I appointed you that ye should go and bear fruit, *that* . . . whatsoever ye shall ask of the Father in my name, he may give it to you."

Let us seek to enter into the spirit of what the Saviour teaches us here. There is a danger in our evangelical religion of looking one-sidedly at this experience of obtaining things in prayer and faith. Another side which God's Word puts very strongly is that obedience is the only path to blessing. We need to realize that in our relationship to the Infinite Being whom we call God, who has created and redeemed us, the first sentiment that ought to animate us is that of subjection. The surrender to His supremacy, His glory, His will, His pleasure, ought to be the first and uppermost thought of our life. The question is not how we are to obtain and enjoy His favor, for in this the main thing may still be self. But what this Being in the very nature of things rightfully claims—and is infinitely and unspeakably worthy of—is that His glory and pleasure should be my one object. Surrender to His perfect and blessed will, a life of service and obedience, is the beauty and the charm of heaven. Service and obedience were the thoughts that were uppermost in the mind of the Son when He dwelt upon earth. Service and obedience must become with us the chief objects of desire and aim, more so than rest or light, or joy or strength; in them we shall find the path to all the higher blessedness that awaits us.

Just note what a prominent place the Master gives it, not only in this fifteenth chapter, in connection with the abiding, but in the fourteenth, where He speaks of the indwelling of the Triune God. In verse 15 we have it: *"If ye* love me, *keep my command-ments,* and the Spirit will be given you of the Father.'' Then verse 21: ''he that hath *my commandments and keepeth them,* he it is that loveth me''; and he shall have the special love of my Father resting on him, and the special manifestation of myself. Then verse 23 gives one of the highest of all the exceedingly great and precious promises: ''If a man love me *he will keep my words,* and the Father and I will come and take up our abode with him.'' Could words put it more clearly that obedience is the way to the indwelling of the Spirit, to His revealing the Son within us, and to His again preparing us to be the abode, the home of the Father?

The indwelling of the Triune God is the heritage of those who obey. Obedience and faith are but two aspects of one act—sur-render to God and His will. As faith strengthens for obedience, it is in turn strengthened by it. Faith is made perfect by works. Too often our efforts to believe have been unavailing because we have not taken up the only position in which strong faith is legitimate or possible—that of entire surrender to the honor and the will of God. The man who is entirely consecrated to God and His will finds power to claim everything that His God has promised to be for him.

The application of this in prayer is very simple, but very sol-emn. ''I chose you,'' the Master says, ''and appointed you that ye should go and bear fruit," much fruit (vv. 5, 8). "And that your fruit should abide," that your life might be one of abiding fruit and abiding fruitfulness. "That" as fruitful branches abiding in me, "whatsoever ye shall ask of the Father in my name, he may give it you." How often we have tried to pray for much grace to bear fruit, and have wondered when the answer did not come. It was because we were reversing the Master's order. We wanted to have the comfort and the joy and the strength first that we might do the work easily and without any feeling of difficulty or self-sacrifice. Only He wanted us in faith—without asking whether we felt weak or strong, whether the work was hard or easy—to do in the obedience of faith what He said. The path of fruit-bearing would have led us to the place and the power of prevailing prayer.

Obedience is the only path that leads to the glory of God. Not obedience instead of faith, nor obedience to supply the shortcomings of faith. Faith's obedience gives access to all the blessings our God has for us. The baptism of the Spirit (14:16), the manifestation of the Son (14:21), the indwelling of the Father (14:23), the abiding in Christ's love (15:10), the privilege of His holy friendship (15:14), and power of all-prevailing prayer (15:16)— all wait the obedient.

What have we learned? We know now the reason why we have not had power to prevail in believing prayer. Our life was not as it should have been. Simple downright obedience, abiding fruitfulness, was not its chief mark. And with our whole heart we approve of the divine appointment: men to whom God is to give such influence in the rule of the world that at their request He will do what otherwise would not have taken place, men whose will is to guide the path in which God's will is to work—but these must be men who have themselves learned obedience, whose loyalty and submission to authority must be above all suspicion. Our whole soul approves the law that obedience and fruit-bearing are the path to prevailing prayer. With shame we acknowledge how little our lives have yet borne this stamp.

Let us yield ourselves to accept and fulfill the appointment the Saviour gives us. Let us study His relation to us as Master. With each new day let us no longer think first of comfort or joy or blessing. Let the first thought be: I belong to the Master. Every moment and in every action I must act as His property, as a part of himself, as one who only seeks to know and do His will. A servant, a slave of Jesus Christ—let this be the spirit that animates me. If He says, "No longer do I call you servants, but I have called you friends," let us accept the place of friends. "Ye are my friends if ye do the things which I command you."

The one thing He commands us as His branches is to bear fruit. Let us live to bless others, to testify of the life and the love there is in Jesus. Let us in faith and obedience give our whole life to that which Jesus chose us for and appointed us to—fruit-bearing. As we think of His electing us to this, and take up our appointment as coming from Him who always gives all He demands, we shall grow strong in the confidence that a life of fruit-bearing, abounding and abiding, is within our reach. And we shall understand why this fruit-bearing alone can be the path to the place of all-prevailing prayer. It is the man who, in obedience to the Christ of God, is proving that he is doing what his Lord wills, for whom the Father will do whatsoever he will: "Whatsoever we ask we receive, because we keep his commandments, and do the things that are pleasing in his sight."

Blessed Master, teach me to understand fully that it is only through the will of God, accepted and acted out in obedience to His commands, that we obtain the power to grasp His will in His promises and appropriate them in our prayers. Teach me that the path of fruit-bearing gives deeper growth of the branch into the Vine, and we attain to that perfect oneness with you in which we ask whatsoever we will.

Lord, reveal to us, we pray, how with all the hosts of heaven, and with you the Son on earth, and with all the men of faith who have glorified you on earth, obedience to God is our highest privilege, because it gives access to oneness with Him in that which is His highest glory—His all-perfect will. Reveal to us, we pray, how, in keeping your commandments and bearing fruit according to your will, our spiritual nature will grow up to the full stature of the perfect man, with power to ask and to receive whatsoever we will.

Lord Jesus, reveal yourself to us, and the reality of your purpose and your power to make these wonderful promises the daily experience of all who utterly yield themselves to you and your words. Amen.

The All-Prevailing Plea

"And whatsoever ye shall ask *in my name*, that will I do . . . If ye shall ask me any thing *in my name*, I will do it . . . That whatsoever ye shall ask of the Father *in my name*, he may give it you . . . Verily, verily I say unto you, whatsoever ye shall ask the Father *in my name*, he will give it you. Hitherto have ye asked nothing *in my name*: ask and ye shall receive . . . At that day ye shall ask *in my name* . . ." (John 14:13, 14; 15:16; 16:23, 24, 26).

Until now the disciples had not asked in the name of Christ nor had He himself ever used the expression. The nearest approach is, "met together in my name." Here in His parting words, He repeats the word unceasingly in connection with those promises of unlimited meaning, *"Whatsoever," "Anything," "What ye will,"* to teach them and us that His name is our only, but also our all-sufficient, plea. The power of prayer and the answer depend on the right use of the name.

What is a person's name? It is that word or expression by which the person is called or known to us. When I mention or hear a name, it calls up before me the whole man—what I know of him, and also the impression he has made on me. The name of a king includes his honor, his power, his kingdom. His name is the symbol of his power. And so each name of God embodies and represents some part of the glory of the unseen One. And the name of Christ is the expression of all He has done and all He is and lives to do as our Mediator.

What does it mean to do a thing in the name of another? It is to come with the power and authority of that other, as his representative and substitute. We know how such use of another's name always presumes a common interest. No one would give another the free use of his name without first being assured that his honor and interest were as safe with that other as with himself.

And what is it when Jesus gives us power over His name, the free use of it, with the assurance that whatever we ask in it will be given to us? The ordinary comparison of one person giving another, on some special occasion, the liberty to ask something in his name comes altogether short here. Jesus solemnly gives to *all* His disciples a general and unlimited power of the free use of His name at *all* times for *all* they desire. He could not do this if He did not know that He could trust us with His interests, that His honor would be safe in our hands. The free use of the name of another is always the token of great confidence, of close union. He who gives his name to another stands aside, to let that other act for him. He who takes the name of another gives up his own as of no value. When I go in the name of another, I deny myself, I take not only his name, but I take him and what he is, instead of my own self and what I am.

Such a use of the name of a person may be in virtue of *a legal union.* A merchant leaving his home and business gives his chief clerk a general power of attorney, by which he can draw thousands of pounds in the merchant's name. The clerk does this not for himself, but only in the interests of the business. Because the merchant knows and trusts him as completely devoted to his interests and business, he dares put his name and property at his command. When the Lord Jesus went to heaven, He left His work, the management of His kingdom on earth, in the hands of His servants. He could not do otherwise than also give them His name to draw all the supplies they needed for the due conduct of His business. And they have the spiritual power to avail themselves of the name of Jesus only to the same extent to which they yield themselves to live completely for the interests and the work of the Master. The use of the name always signifies the surrender of our interests to Him whom we represent.

Or such a use of the name may be because of a *life union*. In the case of the merchant and his clerk, the union is temporary. But we know how oneness of life on earth gives oneness of name. A child has the father's name because he has his life. Often the child of a good father has been honored or helped by others for the sake of the name he bore. But this would not last long if it were found that it was only a name and that the father's character was wanting. The name and the character or spirit must be in harmony. When such is the case, the child will have a double claim on the father's friends; the character secures and increases the love and esteem rendered first for the name's sake. So it is with Jesus and the believer: We are one. We have one life, one Spirit with Him, and for this reason we may come in His name. Our power in using that name, whether with God or men or devils, *depends on the measure of our spiritual life union.* The use of the name rests on the unity life; the name and the Spirit of Jesus are one.[1]

Or the union that empowers to the use of the name may be *the union of love.* When a bride whose life has been one of poverty becomes united to the bridegroom, she gives up her own name to be called by his, and then has the full right to use it. She purchases in his name and is not refused. This is done because the bridegroom has chosen her for himself, counting on her to care for his interests. They are now one. The Heavenly Bridegroom could do nothing less. Having loved us and made us one with himself, what could He do but give those who bear His name the right to come with it or present it before the Father for all they need. No one who gives himself really to live in the name of Jesus fails to receive in ever-increasing measure the spiritual capacity to ask and receive in that *name* what he will. The bearing of the name of another supposes my having given up my own name and my own independent life; but it shows just as surely my possession of all there is in the name I have taken instead of my own.

Some illustrations show us how far short the common view falls, ones that picture a messenger sent to ask in the name of another, or a guilty one appealing to the name of a surety. But Jesus himself is with the Father. It is not an absent one in whose name we come. Even when we pray to Jesus himself, it must be in His name. The name represents the person. To ask in the name is to ask in full union of interest and life and love with Him, as one who lives in and for Him. Let the name of Jesus only have undivided supremacy in my heart and life and my faith will grow in assurance that what I ask in that name cannot be refused. The name and power to ask go together. When the name of Jesus has become the power that rules my life, then its power in prayer with God will be seen too.

So we see that everything depends on our own relation to the name. The power it has on my life is the power it will have in my prayers. More than one expression in Scripture clarifies this. When it says, *"Do all* in the name of the Lord Jesus," we see how this is the counterpart of the other, *"Ask all."* To do all and to ask all in His name go together. When we read, "We shall walk in the name of our God," we see how the power of the name must rule in the whole life. Only then will it have power in prayer. God looks not to the lips but to the life to see what the name is to us. When Scripture speaks of "men who have given their lives for the name of the Lord Jesus," or of one "ready to die for the name of the Lord Jesus," we see what our relation to the name must be. When it is everything to me, it will obtain everything for me. If I let it have all I have, it will let me have all it has.

"Whatsoever ye shall ask in my name, that will I do." Jesus means the promise literally. Christians have tried to limit it. It looked too free. It was hardly safe to trust man so unconditionally. We did not understand that the word "in my name" is its own safeguard. It is a spiritual power which no one can use further than he obtains the capacity for, by his living and acting in that name. As we bear that name before men, we have power to use it before God. Plead for God's Holy Spirit to show us what the name means, and what the right use of it is. Through the Spirit the name, which is above every name in heaven, will reign supreme in our heart and life too.

Disciples of Jesus, let these lessons enter deep into your hearts. The Master says: Only pray in my name; whatsoever ye ask will be given. Heaven is opened to you; the treasures and powers of the world of spirit are placed at your disposal on behalf of men around you. Let us learn to pray in the name of Jesus. As to the disciples, He says to us, "Hitherto ye have not asked in my name: ask, and ye shall receive." Let each disciple of Jesus avail himself of the rights of his royal priesthood, and use the power placed at his disposal for his circle and his work. Let Christians wake up and hear the message: your prayer can obtain what otherwise will be withheld, can accomplish what otherwise remains undone. Use the name of Jesus to open the treasures of heaven for this perishing world. Learn as the servants of the King to use His name: "Whatsoever ye shall ask in my name, that will I do."

Blessed Lord, it seems as if each lesson you give me has such fullness and depths of meaning, that I think if I can only learn that one, I shall truly know how to pray. Again I feel as if I need only one prayer: Lord, teach me what it is to pray in your name. Teach me to live and act, to walk and speak, to do all in the name of Jesus, that my prayer will be only in that blessed name too.

Teach me, Lord, to hold fast the precious promise that whatsoever we ask in your name, you will do and the Father will give. Though I do not yet fully understand, and still less have fully attained the wonderful union you mean when you say, "in my name," I would still cling to the promise until it fills my heart with the undoubting assurance: Anything in the name of Jesus.

Lord, let your Holy Spirit teach me this. You called Him, "The Comforter, whom the Father shall send in my name." He knows what it is to be sent from heaven in your name, to reveal and to honor the power of that name in your servants, to use that name alone, and so to glorify you. Lord Jesus, let your Spirit dwell in me and fill me. I would, I do yield my whole being to His rule and leading. Your name and your Spirit are one; through Him your name will be the strength of my life and my prayer. Then I shall be able for your name's sake to forsake all, in your name to speak to men and to God, and to prove that this is indeed the NAME above every name.

Lord Jesus, teach me by your Holy Spirit to pray in your name. Amen.

NOTE

What is meant by praying in Christ's name? It cannot mean simply appearing before God with faith in the mediation of the Saviour. When the disciples asked Jesus to teach them to pray, He supplied them with petitions. And afterward Jesus said to them, 'Hitherto have ye asked nothing in my name.' Until the Spirit came, the seven petitions of the Lord's Prayer lay as it were dormant within them. When by the Holy Ghost Christ descended into their hearts, they desired the very blessings which Christ as our High Priest obtains for us by His prayer from the Father. And such petitions are always answered. The Father is always willing to give what Christ asks. The Spirit of Christ always teaches and influences us to offer the petitions which Christ ratifies and presents to the Father. To pray in Christ's name is therefore to be identified with Christ as our righteousness, and *to be identified with Christ in our desire by the indwelling of the Holy Ghost.* To pray *in the Spirit,* to pray *according to the will of the Father,* to pray *in Christ's name, are identical expressions.* The Father himself loveth us, and is willing to hear us: two intercessors, Christ the Advocate above, and the Holy Ghost, the Advocate within, are the gifts of His love.

This view may appear at first less consoling than a more prevalent one, which refers prayer in Christ's name chiefly to our trust in Christ's merit. The defect of this opinion is, that it does not combine the intercession of the Saviour with the will of the Father, and the indwelling Spirit's aid in prayer. Nor does it fully realize the mediation of Christ; for the mediation consists not merely in that for Christ's sake the Holy Father is able to regard me and my prayer; but also, in that Christ himself presents my petitions as His petitions, desired by Him for me, even as all blessings are purchased for me by His precious blood.

In all prayer, the one essential condition is that we are able to offer it in the name of Jesus, as according to His desire for us, according to the Father's will, according to the Spirit's teaching. And thus praying in Christ's name is impossible without self-examination, without reflection, without self-denial; in short, without the aid of the Spirit.—Saphir, *The Lord's Prayer*

---

[1]"Whatsoever ye shall ask in my name," that is, in my nature; for things with God are called according to their nature. We ask in Christ's name, not when at the end of some request we say, "This I ask in the name of Jesus Christ," but when we pray *according to His nature*, which is love, which seeketh not its own, but only the will of God and the good of all creatures. Such asking is the cry of His own Spirit in our hearts.—Jukes, *The New Man*.

LESSON TWENTY-FIVE

The Holy Spirit and Prayer

"And in that day ye shall ask me nothing. Verily, verily, I say unto you, *Whatsoever ye shall ask* the Father in my name, he will give it you. *Hitherto* have ye ask nothing in my name: ask, and *ye shall receive*, that your joy may be full. *At that day* ye shall ask in my name: and I say not unto you, that I will pray the Father for you; for the Father himself loveth you . . ." (John 16:23, 24, 26, 27).

"Praying in the Holy Ghost, keep yourselves in the love of God" (Jude 20, 21).

The words in 1 John 2:12-14 to little children, to young men and to fathers, suggest the thought that often in the Christian life there are three great stages of experience. The first is that of the newborn child, with the assurances and the joy of forgiveness. The second is the transition stage of struggle and growth in knowledge and strength: young men growing strong, God's Word doing its work in them and giving them victory over the Evil One. And then there is the final stage of maturity and ripeness: the fathers, who have entered deeply into the knowledge and fellowship of the Eternal One.

In Christ's teaching on prayer there appear to be three stages in the prayer life, somewhat analogous.

In the Sermon on the Mount we have the initial stage: His

teaching is all comprised in one word, Father. Pray to your Father, your Father sees, hears, knows, and will reward—How much more than any earthly father! Only be childlike and trustful.

Then later on comes something like the transition stage of conflict and conquest, in words like these: "This sort goeth not out but by fasting and prayer"; "Shall not God avenge his own elect who cry day and night unto him?"

And then we have a higher stage in the parting words. The children have become men. They are now the Master's friends, from whom He has no secrets, and to whom He says, "All things that I heard from my Father I made known unto you"; and to whom, in the oft-repeated "whatsoever ye will," He hands over the keys of the kingdom. Now the time has come for the power of prayer in His name to be proved.

The contrast between this final stage and the previous preparatory ones our Saviour marks distinctly in the words we are to meditate on: "*Hitherto* ye have asked nothing in my name"; "*At that day* ye shall ask in my name." We know what "*at that day*" means. It is the day of the outpouring of the Holy Spirit. The great work Christ was to do on the cross, the mighty power and the complete victory to be manifested in His resurrection and ascension, were to lead to the coming down from heaven, as never before, of the glory of God to dwell in men. The Spirit of the glorified Jesus was to come and be the life of His disciples. And one of the marks of that wonderful spirit dispensation was to be a power in prayer hitherto unknown—prayer in the name of Jesus, asking and obtaining whatsoever they would to manifest the reality of the Spirit's indwelling.

To understand how the coming of the Holy Spirit was indeed to begin a new epoch in the prayer-world, we must remember who He is, what His work is, and the significance of His not being given until Jesus was glorified. It is in the Spirit that God exists, for He is Spirit. It is in the Spirit that the Son was begotten of the Father. It is in the fellowship of the Spirit that the Father and the Son are one. The eternal never-ceasing giving to the Son which is the Father's prerogative, and the eternal asking and receiving which is the Son's right and blessedness—it is through the Spirit that this communion of life and love is maintained. It has been so from all eternity. It is especially so now, when the Son as Mediator ever lives to pray. The great work of reconciling in His own body God and man which Jesus began on earth, He carries on in heaven. To accomplish this He took up into His own person the conflict betwen God's righteousness and our sin. In His own body on the cross, He once for all ended the struggle. And then He ascended to heaven, that from there He might in each member of His body carry out the deliverance and manifest the victory He had obtained. To do this, He ever lives to pray. In His unceasing intercession, He places himself in living fellowship with the unceasing prayer of His redeemed ones. Or rather, it is His unceasing intercession which shows itself in their prayers, and gives them a power they never had before.

He does this through the Holy Spirit. The Holy Spirit, the Spirit of the glorified Jesus, was not (John 7:39), could not be, until He had been glorified. This gift of the Father was something distinctively new, entirely different from what Old Testament saints had known. The work that the blood effected in heaven when Christ entered within the veil was something true and new. The redemption of our human nature into fellowship with His resurrection power and His exaltation glory was so intensely real, the taking up of our humanity in Christ into the life of the Triune God was an event of such inconceivable significance, that the Holy Spirit, who had to come from Christ's exalted humanity to testify in our hearts of what Christ had accomplished, was no longer only what He had been in the Old Testament. It was literally true "the Holy Spirit was not yet, for Christ was not yet glorified." He came now first as the Spirit of the glorified Jesus. The Son, who from eternity was God, had entered upon a new existence as man, and returned to heaven with what He did not have before. So the Blessed Spirit, whom the Son on His ascension received from the Father into His glorified humanity (Acts 2:33) also came to us with a new life which He previously did not have to communicate. Under the Old Testament He was invoked as the Spirit of God. At Pentecost He descended as the Spirit of the glorified Jesus, bringing down and communicating to us the full fruit and power of the accomplished redemption.

In the intercession of Christ, the continued efficacy and application of His redemption is maintained. Through the Holy Spirit descending from Christ to us, we are drawn up into the great stream of His ever-ascending prayers. The Spirit prays for us without words. In the depths of a heart where even thoughts are at times formless, the Spirit takes us up into the wonderful flow of the life of the Triune God. Through the Spirit, Christ's prayers become ours, and ours are made His; we ask what we will, and it is given to us. We then understand from experience, "Hitherto ye have asked nothing in my name. *At that day* ye shall ask in my name."

What we need to pray in the name of Christ, to ask that we may receive that our joy may be full, is the baptism of this Holy Spirit. This is more than the Spirit of God under the Old Testament. This is more than the Spirit of conversion and regeneration the disciples had before Pentecost. This is more than the Spirit with a measure of His influence and working. This is the Holy Spirit, the Spirit of the glorified Jesus in His exaltation power, coming on us as the Spirit of the indwelling Jesus, revealing the Son and the Father within (John 14:16-23). When this Spirit is the Spirit not only of our hours of prayer, but of our whole life and walk; when this Spirit glorifies Jesus in us by revealing the completeness of His work, making us wholly one with Him and like Him; then we can pray in His name, because we are in very deed one with Him. Then it is that we have that instant access to the Father of which Jesus says, "I say not that I will pray the Father for you."

How we need to understand and believe that to be filled with this Spirit of the glorified One is the one need of God's believing people! Then we shall understand "with all prayer and supplication to be praying at all seasons in the Spirit," and "praying in the Holy Spirit, to keep ourselves in love of God." "*At that day* ye shall ask in my name."

Once again we see that what our prayer avails depends upon what we are and what our life is. Living in the name of Christ is the secret of praying in the name of Christ. Living in the Spirit fits one for praying in the Spirit. Abiding in Christ gives the right and power to ask what we will. The extent of the abiding is the exact measure of the power in prayer. The Spirit dwelling within us prays, not in words and thoughts always, but in a breathing and a being deeper than utterance. According to how much there is of Christ's Spirit in us, is there real prayer. If our lives be full of Christ and full of His Spirit, the wonderfully unlimited promises to our prayer will no longer be rare or unusual. "Hitherto ye have asked nothing in my name. Ask, and ye shall receive, that your joy may be full. At that day ye shall ask in my name. Verily verily, I say unto you, Whatsoever ye shall ask the Father in my name, he will give it you."

In holy awe I bow before you, the Triune God. Again I have seen how the mystery of prayer is the mystery of the Holy Trinity. I adore the Father who ever hears, and the Son who ever lives to pray, and the Holy Spirit, proceeding from the Father and the Son, to lift us up into the fellowship of that ever-blessed, never-ceasing asking and receiving. I bow, my God, in adoring worship before this infinite condescension that through the Holy Spirit, takes us and our prayers into the divine life and its fellowship of love.

Blessed Lord Jesus, teach me to understand your lesson, that it is the indwelling Spirit, streaming from you and uniting to you who is the Spirit of prayer. Teach me what it is as an empty, wholly consecrated vessel, to yield myself to His being my life. Teach me to honor and trust Him as a living person, to lead my life and my prayer. Teach me to wait in holy silence in prayer and give Him place to breathe within me His unutterable intercession. Teach me that through Him it is possible to pray without ceasing—and to pray without failing—because He makes me partaker of the never-ceasing and never-failing intercession in which you, the Son, appear before the Father. Yea, Lord, fulfill in me your promise, "At that day ye shall ask in my name. Verily, verily, I say unto you, Whatsoever ye shall ask the Father in my name, He will give it you." Amen.

NOTE

Prayer has often been compared to breathing: we have only to carry out the comparison fully to see how wonderful the place is which the Holy Spirit occupies. With every breath we expel the impure air which would soon cause our death, and inhale again the fresh air to which we owe our life. So we give out the sins in confession and the needs and the desires of our heart in prayer. Drawing in our breath again, we inhale the fresh air of the promises, the love and the life of God in Christ. We do this through the Holy Spirit, who is the breathe of our life.

And this He is because He is the breathe of God. The Father breathes Him into us to unite Him with our life. Just as on every expiration there follows again the inhaling or drawing in of the breath, so God draws in again His breath, and the Spirit returns to Him laden with the desires and needs of our hearts. Thus the Holy Spirit is the breath of the life of God and the breath of the new life in us. As God breathes Him out, we receive Him in answer to prayer: as we breathe Him back again, He rises to God laden with our supplications. As the Spirit of God, in whom the Father and the Son are one, and the intercession of the Son reaches the Father, He is to us the Spirit of prayer. True prayer is the living experience of the truth of the Holy Trinity. The Spirit's breathing, the Son's intercession, the Father's will—these three become one in us.

Christ the Intercessor

"But I have prayed for thee, that thy faith fail not" (Luke 22:32).

"I say not unto you, that I will pray the Father for you" (John 16:26).

"He ever liveth to make intercession" (Heb. 7:25).

All growth in the spiritual life is connected with a clearer insight into what Jesus is to us. The more I realize that Christ must be all to me and in me and that all in Christ is indeed for me, the more I learn to live the real life of faith, which in dying to self, lives wholly in Christ. The Christian life is no longer the vain struggle to live right, but the resting in Christ and finding strength in Him as our life, to fight the fight and gain the victory of faith. This is especially true of the life of prayer. As it too comes under the law of faith alone, and is seen in the light of the fullness and completeness there is in Jesus, the believer understands that it need no longer be a matter of strain or anxious care, but an experience of what Christ will do for him and in him. Further, it will be a participation in that life of Christ which, on earth as in heaven, ever ascends to the Father as prayer. He begins to pray, not only trusting in the merits of Jesus or in the intercession by which our unworthy prayers are made acceptable, but in that near and close union by which He prays in us and we in Him.[1] The whole of salvation is Christ himself. He has given himself to us. He himself lives in us. Because He prays, we pray too. Just as the disciples, when they saw Jesus pray, asked Him to make them partakers of what He knew of prayer, so we, seeing Him as intercessor on the throne, know that He makes us participate with Him in the life of prayer.

How clearly this comes out in the last night of His life. In His high-priestly prayer (John 17), He shows us how and what He has to pray to the Father, and will pray when once ascended to heaven. But in His parting address He repeatedly connected His going to the Father with *their* new life of prayer. The two would be ultimately connected. His entrance into the work of His eternal intercession *would be the commencement and the power of their new prayer life in His name.* It is the sight of Jesus in His intercession that gives us power to pray in His name. All right and power of prayer is Christ's. He makes us share in His intercession.

To understand this, think first of *His intercession*. He ever lives to make intercession. The work of Christ on earth as Priest was but a beginning. It was as Aaron He shed His blood. It is as Melchizedek that He now lives within the veil to continue His work, after the power of the eternal life. As Melchizedek is more glorious than Aaron, so it is in the work of intercession that the atonement has its true power and glory. "It is Christ that died: *yea more,* who is even at the right hand of God, who maketh intercession for us." That intercession is an intense reality, a work that is absolutely necessary, and without which the continued application of redemption cannot take place.

In the incarnation and resurrection of Jesus the wonderful reconciliation took place, by which man became partaker of the divine life and blessedness. But the real personal appropriation of this reconciliation in each of His members here below cannot take place without the unceasing exercise of His divine power by the head in heaven. In all conversion and sanctification, in every victory over sin and the world, there is a real putting forth of the power of Him who is mighty to save. This exercise of His power only takes place through His prayer. He asks of the Father, and receives from the Father. *"He is able* to save to the uttermost, *because* he ever liveth to make intercession." There is never a need of His people without Him receiving in intercession what the Godhead has to give. His mediation on the throne is as real and indispensable as on the cross. Nothing takes place without His intercession. It engages all His time and powers. It is His unceasing occupation at the right hand of the Father.

We participate not only in the benefits of this His work, but in the work itself—because we are His body. Body and members are one. "The head cannot say to the feet, I have no need of thee." We share with Jesus in all He is and has. "The glory which thou gavest me, I have given them." We are partakers of His life, His righteousness, His work; we share with Him in His intercession too; it is not a work He does without us.

We do this because we are partakers of His life. "Christ is our life"; "No longer I, but Christ liveth in me." The life in Him and in us is identical, one and the same. His life in heaven is an *ever-praying* life. When it descends and takes possession of us, it does not lose its character. In us too it is the *ever-praying* life—a life that without ceasing asks and receives from God. It is not as if there were two separate currents of prayer rising upward, one from Him, and one from His people. No, but the substantial life-union is also prayer-union: what He prays passes through us, what we pray passes through Him. He is the angel with the golden censer: "Unto him there was given much incense," the secret of acceptable prayer, "that he should add it unto the prayers of all the saints upon the golden altar." We live, we abide in Him, the interceding One.

The Only-begotten is the only one who has the right to pray. To Him alone it was said, "Ask, and it shall be given thee." As in all other things the fullness dwells in Him, so does the true prayerfulness too; He alone has the power of prayer. Just as the growth of the spiritual life consists in the clearer insight that all the treasures are *in Him*, and that we too are *in Him*, to receive each moment what we possess in Him, grace for grace, so it is with the prayer life too. Our faith in the intercession of Jesus must not only be that He prays in our place, when we do not or cannot pray, but that, as the Author of our life and our faith, He leads us to pray in unison with himself. Our prayer must be a work of faith in this sense also. Just as Jesus communicates His whole life in us, He also out of that prayerfulness which is His alone breathes into us our praying.

To many a believer it was a new epoch in his spiritual life when it was revealed to him how truly and entirely Christ was his life, standing good as the guarantee for his remaining faithful and obedient. It was then that he first really began to live a *faith-life*. No less blessed will be the discovery that Christ is the guarantee for our prayer life too, the center and embodiment of all prayer, to be communicated by Him through the Holy Spirit to His people.

"He ever liveth to make intercession" as the Head of the body, as the Leader in that new and living way which He has opened up, as the Author and the Perfecter of our faith. He provides everything for the life of His redeemed ones by giving His own life in them. He cares for their life of prayer, by taking them up into His heavenly prayer life, by giving and maintaining His prayer life within them. "I have prayed for thee," not to render our faith needless, but "that *thy faith* fail not." Our faith and prayer of faith is rooted in His. It is, "if ye abide in me," the everliving Intercessor, and pray with me and in me, "ask whatsoever ye will, and it shall be done unto you."

The thought of our fellowship in the intercession of Jesus reminds us of what He has taught us more than once before, how all these wonderful prayer promises have as their aim and their justification, the glory of God in the manifestation of His kingdom and the salvation of sinners. As long as we only or mainly pray for ourselves, the promises of the last night must remain a sealed book to us. It is to the fruit-bearing branches of the Vine; it is to disciples sent into the world as the Father sent Him, to live for perishing men; it is to His faithful servants and intimate friends who take up the work He leaves behind, who like their Lord have become as seed corn, losing its life to multiply it manifold—to such the promises are given. Let us each find out what the work is, and which souls are entrusted to our special prayers. Let us make our intercession for them our life of fellowship with God, and we shall not only find the promises of power in prayer proven true to us, but we shall then see how our abiding in Christ and His abiding in us make us share in His own joy of blessing and saving men.

How wonderful is this intercession of our Blessed Lord Jesus, to which we not only owe everything, but in which we are taken up as active partners and fellow workers! Now we understand what it is to pray in the name of Jesus, and why it has such power. In His name, in His Spirit, in perfect union with Him. This wonderful, ever-active, and most efficacious intercession of the man Christ Jesus—when shall we be wholly caught up into it, and always pray in it?

Blessed Lord, in adoration I would again bow before you. Your whole redemption work has now passed into prayer. All that now occupies you in maintaining and dispensing what you purchased with your blood is only prayer. You ever live to pray. Because we abide in you the direct access to the Father is always open. Our life can be one of unceasing prayer. The answer to our prayer is assured.

Blessed Lord, you have invited your people to be your fellow workers in a life of prayer. You have united yourself with your people and make them as your body share with you in that ministry of intercession through which alone the world can be filled with the fruit of your redemption and the glory of the Father. With more liberty than ever I come to you, my Lord, and beseech you: Teach me to pray. Your life is prayer, your life is mine. Lord! Teach me to pray, in you, like you.

Lord, help me to know, as you promise your disciples, that you are in the Father, and I in you, and you in me. Let the uniting power of the Holy Spirit make my whole life an abiding in you and your intercession, so that my prayer may be its echo, and the Father hear me in you and you in me. Lord Jesus, let your mind in everything be in me, and my life in everything be in you. So shall I be prepared to be the channel through which your intercession pours its blessing on the world. Amen.

NOTE

The new epoch of prayer in the name of Jesus is pointed out

by Christ as the time of the outpouring of the Spirit, in which the disciples enter upon a more enlightened apprehension of the economy of redemption, and become as clearly conscious of their oneness with Jesus as of His oneness with the Father. Their prayer in the name of Jesus is now directed to the Father himself. "*I say not that I will pray* for you, for the Father himself loveth you," Jesus says; while He had previously spoken of the time before the Spirit's coming: "*I will pray* the Father, and he will give you the Comforter." This prayer thus has as its center thought the insight into our being united to God in Christ as on both sides the living bond of union between God and us (John 17:23: "I in them and thou in me"), so that in Jesus we behold the Father as united to us, and ourselves as united to the Father. Jesus Christ must have been revealed to us, not only through the truth in the mind, but in our inmost personal consciousness as the living personal reconciliation, as He in whom God's Fatherhood and Father-love have been perfectly united with human nature and it with God. Not that with the immediate prayer to the Father, the mediatorship of Christ is set aside; but it is no longer looked at as something external, existing outside of us, but as a real living spiritual existence within us, so that the Christ *for us*, the Mediator, has really become Christ *in us*.

When the consciousness of this oneness between God in Christ and us in Christ still is waning, or has been darkened by the sense of guilt, then, the prayer of faith looks to our Lord as the Advocate, who prays the Father *for us*. (Compare John 16:26 with 14:16, 17; 9:20; Luke 22:32; 1 John 2:1.) To take Christ thus in prayer as Advocate is according to John 16:26 not perfectly the same as the prayer in His name.

Christ's advocacy is meant to lead us on to that inner self-standing life-union with Him, and with the Father in Him, in virtue of which Christ is He in whom God enters into immediate relation and unites himself with us, and in whom we in all circumstances enter into immediate relation with God. Even so the prayer in the name of Jesus does not consist in our prayer at His command: the disciples had prayed thus ever since the Lord had given them His "Our Father," and yet He says, "Hitherto ye have not prayed in my name." Only when the mediation of

Christ has become, through the indwelling of the Holy Spirit, life and power within us, and so *His mind, as it found expression in His word and work, has taken possession of and filled our personal consciousness and will,* so that in faith and love we have Jesus in us as the Reconciler who has actually made us one with God, only then His name, which includes His nature and His work, is become truth and power in us (not only for us), and we have in the name of Jesus the free, direct access to the Father which is sure of being heard.

Prayer in the name of Jesus is the liberty of a son with the Father, just as Jesus had this as the First-begotten. We pray in the place of Jesus, not as if we could put ourselves in His place, but insofar as we are in Him and He in us. We go directly to the Father, but only as the Father is in Christ, not as if He were separate from Christ. Wherever thus the inner man does not live in Christ, and has Him not present as the Living One, where His word is not ruling in the heart in its Spirit-power, where His truth and life have not become the life of our soul, it is vain to think that a formula like "for the sake of thy dear Son" will avail.—*Christliche Ethik,* von Dr. I. T. Beck, Tubingen.

---

[1]See the difference between having Christ as an Advocate or Intercessor who stands outside of us, and the having Him within us, we abiding in Him and He in us through the Holy Spirit perfecting our union with Him, so that we ourselves can come directly to the Father in His name.—The note from Beck of Tubingen.

Christat the High Priest

"Father, I will that they also, whom thou hast given me, be with me where I am" (John 17:24).

In His parting address, Jesus gives His disciples the full revelation of what the new life was to be, when once the kingdom of God had come in power. In the indwelling of the Holy Spirit, in union with Him, the heavenly Vine, in their going forth to witness and to suffer for Him, they were to find their calling and their blessedness. In between His telling of their future new life, the Lord had repeatedly given the most unlimited promises as to the power their prayers might have.

In closing, He himself proceeds to pray. To let His disciples have the joy of knowing what His intercession for them in heaven as their High Priest will be, He gives this precious legacy of His prayer to the Father. He does this at the same time because they as priests are to share in His work of intercession, that they and we might know how to perform this holy work. In the teaching of our Lord on this last night, we have learned to understand that these astonishing prayer promises have not been given in our own behalf, but in the interest of the Lord and His kingdom. From the Lord alone can we learn what the prayer in His name is to be and to obtain. We saw that to pray in His name is to pray in perfect unity with Him. The high-priestly prayer will teach all that the prayer in the name of Jesus may ask and expect.

This prayer is ordinarily divided into three parts. Our Lord first prays for himself (5:1-5), then for His disciples (6-19), and last for all the believing people through all ages (20-26). The follower of Jesus, who dedicates himself to the work of intercession and wants to pray down blessing upon his circle in the name of Jesus, will submit humbly to the guidance of the Spirit and study this wonderful prayer as one of the most important prayer lessons.

First, Jesus prays for himself, to be glorified so that He may glorify the Father. "Father, glorify thy Son. And now, Father, glorify me." He shows the grounds on which He prays. A holy covenant had been concluded between the Father and the Son in heaven. The Father had promised Him power over all flesh as the reward of His work. He had done the work, He had glorified the Father, and His one purpose is now to glorify Him still further. With utmost boldness He asks that the Father may glorify Him, that He may now be and do for His people all He has undertaken.

Disciple of Jesus, here is the first lesson in your work of priestly intercession, to be learned from the example of your great High Priest. To pray in the name of Jesus is to pray in unity, in sympathy with Him. The Son began His prayer by making clear His relation to the Father, pleading His work and obedience and His desire to see the Father glorifed. Do the same. Draw near to appear before the Father in Christ. Plead His finished work. Say that you are one with it, that you trust on it, live in it. Say that you too have given yourself to finish the work the Father has given you to do and to live alone for His glory. Then confidently ask that the Son may be glorified in you.

This is praying in the name, in the very words, in the Spirit of Jesus, in union with Jesus himself. Such prayer has power. If with Jesus you glorify the Father, the Father will glorify Jesus by doing what you ask in His name. It is only when your own personal relation on this point, like Christ's, is clear with God, when you are glorifying Him, and seeking all for His glory, that, like Christ, you will have power to intercede for those around you.

Our Lord next prays for the circle of His disciples. He speaks of them as those whom the Father has given Him. Their distinguishing mark is that they have received Christ's word. He says of them that He now sends them into the world in His place, just as the Father has sent Him. He asks two things for them: that the Father keep them from the evil one, and sanctify them through His Word, because He sanctifies himself for them.

Just like the Lord, each believing intercessor has his own immediate circle for whom he first prays. Parents have their children, teachers their pupils, pastors their flocks, all workers their special charge, all believers those whose care lies upon their hearts. It is essential that intercession should be personal, pointed, and definite. Our first prayer must always be that they may receive the Word. But this prayer will not avail unless with our Lord we say, "I have given them thy word." This gives us liberty and power in intercession for souls—not only to pray for them, but speak to them. And when they have received the word, let us pray much for their being kept from the evil one and for them to be sanctified through that word. Instead of being hopeless or judging or giving up those who fall, let us pray for our circle, "Father, keep them in thy name"; "Sanctify them through thy truth." Prayer in the name of Jesus avails much: "What ye will shall be done unto you."

Then follows our Lord's prayer for a still wider circle. "I pray not only for these, but for them who through their word shall believe." His priestly heart enlarges itself to embrace all places and all time, and He prays that all who belong to Him may everywhere be one, as God's proof to the world of the divinity of His mission, and then that they may ever be with Him in His glory. Until then "that the love wherewith thou hast loved me may be in them, and I in them."

The disciple of Jesus, who has first in his own circle proved the power of prayer, cannot confine himself within its limits. He prays for the Church universal and its different branches. He prays especially for the unity of the Spirit and of love. He prays for its being one in Christ, as a witness to the world that Christ, who wonderfully made love triumph over selfishness and separation, is indeed the Son of God sent from heaven. Every believer ought to pray much that the unity of the Church—not in external organizations, but in spirit and in truth—may be made manifest.

So much for the matter of the prayer. Now for its mode. Jesus says, "Father, I will." On the ground of His right as Son, and the Father's promise to Him, and His finished work, He was able to do so. The Father had said to Him, "Ask of me, and I will give thee." He simply availed himself of the Father's promise. Jesus has given us a like promise: *"Whatsoever ye will* shall be done unto you."* He asks me in His name to say what I will.

Abiding in Him, in a living union with Him in which man is nothing and Christ all, the believer has the liberty to take up the word of His High Priest. In answer to the question. *"What wilt thou?"* he is able to say, "Father, I *will* all that you have promised."* This is true faith. This honors God, to be assured that such confidence in saying what I will is indeed acceptable to Him. At first sight, our heart shrinks from the expression. We feel neither the liberty nor the power to speak like this. It is a word for which alone, in the most entire abnegation of our will, grace will be given, but for which grace will most assuredly be given to each one who loses his will in his Lord's. He that loses his will shall find it; he that gives up his will entirely shall find it again renewed and strengthened with a divine strength. "Father, I will:" this is the keynote of the everlasting, ever-active, all-prevailing intercession of our Lord in heaven. It is only in union with Him that our prayer avails; in union with Him it avails much.

If we but abide in Him, living, and walking, and doing all things in His name; if we but come and bring each separate petition, tested and touched by His Word and Spirit, and cast it into the mighty stream of intercession that goes up from Him, to be borne upward and presented before the Father—then we shall have the full confidence that we receive the petitions we ask. The "Father, *I will*" will be breathed into us by the Spirit himself. We shall lose ourselves in Him, and become nothing, to find that in our impotence we have power and prevail.

Disciples of Jesus, called to be like your Lord in His priestly intercession, when shall we be like Him? When shall we awaken to the glory—passing all conception—of our destiny to plead and prevail with God for perishing men? When shall we shake off the sloth that masks itself with a pretense of humility? Let us yield ourselves wholly to God's Spirit, that He may fill our wills with light and with power, to know, to take, and to possess all that our God is waiting to give to a will that takes hold of Him.

Blessed High Priest, who am I that you should invite me to share with you in your power of prevailing intercession? Why, Lord, am I so slow to understand and believe, to exercise this wonderful privilege to which you have redeemed your people? Lord, give your grace that this may increasingly be my unceasing life-work—to pray without ceasing to bring the blessing of heaven down on all around me on earth.

Lord, I come to accept this my calling. For this I would forsake all and follow you. Into your hands I would yield my whole being in believing trust. Form and train me to be one of your prayer legion. Inspire me to be one with the wrestlers who watch and strive in prayer, Israels, God's princes, who have power and prevail. Take possession of my heart, and fill it with one desire— the glory of God in the ingathering, sanctification, and union of those whom the Father has given you. Take my mind and let this be my study and my wisdom, to know when prayer can bring a blessing. Take me wholly and fit me as a priest to stand always before God and to bless in His name.

Blessed Lord, may it be here, as through all the spiritual life: you all, I nothing. May it be my experience that he that has and seeks nothing for himself receives all, even to the wonderful grace of sharing with you in your everlasting ministry of intercession. Amen.

Christ the Sacrifice

"And he said, Abba, Father, all things are possible unto thee; take away this cup from me: nevertheless not what I will, but what thou wilt" (Mark 14:36).

What a contrast within the space of a few hours! What a transition from the quiet elevation of, "He lifted up his eyes to heaven, and said, Father! I will," to falling on the ground and crying in agony, "My Father! not what I will." In the one we see the High Priest within the veil in His all-prevailing intercession; in the other, the sacrifice on the altar opening the way through the rent veil. In order of time the high priestly "Father! I will" precedes the sacrificial "Father! not what I will"; but this was only to show beforehand what the intercession would be when once the sacrifice was brought. In reality it was that prayer at the altar, "Father! not what I will," in which the prayer before the throne, "Father! I will," had its origin and its power. Because of the entire surrender of His will in Gethsemane, the High Priest on the throne has the power to ask what He will. He has the right to make His people share in that power too, and ask what they will.

This Gethsemane lesson is one of the most sacred and precious of all. To a superficial learner it may appear to take away the courage to pray in faith. If even the earnest supplication of the Son was not heard, if even He had to say, "Not what I will!" how much more do we need to speak so? Now it appears impossible that the promises which the Lord had given only a few hours previously, "Whatsoever ye shall ask," "Whatsoever ye will," could have been meant literally. A deeper insight into the meaning of Gethsemane would teach us that it is precisely here we have sure ground and an open way to assurance of an answer to our prayer. Let us draw near in reverent and adoring wonder, to gaze on this great sight of God's Son offering up prayer and supplications with strong crying and tears—and not obtaining what He asks. He himself is our Teacher and will open up to us the mystery of His holy sacrifice as revealed in this awesome prayer.

To understand the prayer, let us note the infinite difference between what our Lord prayed a little while ago as a Royal High Priest, and what He begs here in His weakness. *There* He prayed for the glorifying of the Father and the glorifying of himself and His people as the fulfillment of distinct promises that had been given Him. What He asked He knew to be according to the word and the will of the Father; He might boldly say, "Father! I will." *Here* He prays for something in regard to which the Father's will is not yet clear to Him. As far as He knows, it is the Father's will that he should drink the cup. He had told His disciples of the cup He must drink. A little later He would again say, "The cup which my Father hath given me, shall I not drink it?" It was for this He had come to this earth.

When the unutterable agony of soul burst upon Him as the power of darkness came upon Him, and He began to taste the first drops of death as the wrath of God against sin, His human nature shuddered in the presence of the awful reality of being made a curse. Then He cried out in anguish desiring that, if God's purpose could be accomplished without it, He might be spared the awful cup: "Let this cup pass from me." That desire was evidence of the intense reality of His humanity. The "not as I will" kept that desire from being sinful. He pleadingly cries, "All things are possible with thee," and returns again to still more earnest prayer that the cup may be removed.

His thrice-repeated "not what I will" constitutes the very

essence and worth of His sacrifice. He had asked for something of which He could not say: I know it is Thy will. He had pleaded God's power and love, and had then withdrawn it in His final, "Thy will be done." The prayer that the cup should pass away could not be answered; the prayer of submission that God's will be done was heard and gloriously, first in His victory over the fear and then over the power of death.

In this denial of His will and this complete surrender of His will to the will of the Father, Christ's obedience reached its highest perfection. From the sacrifice of the will in Gethsemane, the sacrifice of the life on Calvary derives its value. As Scripture says, He learned obedience here and became the author of everlasting salvation to all that obey Him. It was because He there, in that prayer, became obedient unto death, even the death of the cross, that God has highly exalted him, and given Him the power to ask what He will. In that "Father, not what I will," He obtained the power for that other, "Father, I will." It was by Christ's submittal in Gethsemane to have not His will done that He secured for His people the right to say to them, "Ask whatsoever ye will."

Gethsemane offers deep mysteries. First: the Father offers His Well-Beloved the cup of wrath. Second: the Son, always so obedient, shrinks back and implores that He may not have to drink it. Third: the Father does not grant the Son His request, but still gives the cup. Then last: the Son yields His will, is content that His will be not done, and goes out to Calvary to drink the cup. Gethsemane, in you I see my Lord could give me such unlimited assurance of an answer to my prayers. As my surety He won it for me, by His consent to have His petition unanswered.

This is in harmony with the whole scheme of redemption. Our Lord always wins for us the opposite of what He suffered. He was bound that we might go free. He was made sin that we might become the righteousness of God. He died that we might go free. He bore God's curse that God's blessing might be ours. He endured the not answering of His prayer that our prayers might find an answer. He said, "Not as I will," that He might say to us, "If ye abide in me, ask what ye will; it shall be done unto you."

Here in Gethsemane the word "if ye abide in me" acquires

new force and depth. Christ is our Head, who as surety stands in our place, and bears what we must have borne forever. We deserved that God should turn a deaf ear to us and never listen to our cry. Christ comes and suffers this too for us. He suffers what we merited. For our sins He suffers beneath the burden of that unanswered prayer. But now His suffering avails for me. His merit has won for me the answer to every prayer if I abide in Him.

I must abide in Him, as He bows there in Gethsemane. As my Head, He not only once suffered for me, but ever lives in me, breathing and working His own nature in me too. The Eternal Spirit, through which He offered himself unto God, is the Spirit that dwells in me too, and makes me partaker of the very same obedience, and the sacrifice of the will unto God. That Spirit teaches me to yield my will entirely to the will of the Father, to give it up even though it be not directly sinful. He teaches me to fear and flee.

The Spirit opens my ear to wait in great gentleness and teachableness of soul for what the Father has day by day to speak and to teach. He shows me how with God's will is union with God himself. He shows me that entire surrender to God's will is the Father's claim, the Son's example, and the true blessedness of the soul. He leads my will into the fellowship of Christ's death and resurrection. My will dies in Him, in Him to be made alive again. He breathes into it, as a renewed and quickened will, a holy insight into God's perfect will, a holy joy in yielding itself to be an instrument of that will. He gives a holy liberty and power to lay hold of God's will to answer prayer. With my whole will I learn to live for the interests of God and His kingdom, to exercise the power of that will—crucified but risen again—in nature and in prayer, on earth and in heaven, with men and with God.

The more deeply I enter into the "Father, not what I will" of Gethsemane, and abide in Him who spake it, the fuller is my spiritual access into the power of His, "Father, I will." Then the soul finds that the will, which has become nothing that God's will may be all, now becomes inspired with a divine strength to truly will what God wills, and to claim what what has been promised it in the name of Christ.

Listen to Christ in Gethsemane as He calls, "If ye abide in me, ask whatsoever ye will, and it shall be done unto you." Being of one mind and spirit with Him in His giving up everything to God's will, living like Him in obedience and surrender to the Father—this is abiding in Him. This is the secret of power in prayer.

Blessed Lord Jesus, Gethsemane was your school, where you learned to pray and to obey. It is still the school where you lead all your disciples who want to learn to obey and to pray like you. Lord, there teach me to pray in faith that you atoned for and conquered our self-will, and can indeed give us grace to pray like you.

Lamb of God, I would follow you to Gethsemane, there to become one with you and to abide in you as you, unto the very death, yielded up your will unto the Father. With you, through you, in you, I do yield my will in absolute and entire surrender to the will of the Father. I claim in faith the power of your victory, conscious of my own weakness, and the secret power with which self-will would assert itself and again take its place on the throne. You did triumph over it and deliver me from it. In your death I would daily live. In your life I would daily die. Abiding in you through the power of your eternal Spirit, let my will only be the tuned instrument which yields to every touch of the will of my God. With my whole soul do I say with you, "Father, not as I will, but as you will."

Then, Blessed Lord, open my heart and that of all your people, to accept fully the glory of the truth that a will given up to God is a will accepted of God to be used in His service, to desire, purpose, determine, and will that which is according to God's will. Then it will be a will which, in the power of the Holy Spirit, the indwelling God, is to exercise its royal prerogative in prayer, to loose and to bind in heaven and upon earth, to ask whatsoever it will, and to say it shall be done.

Lord Jesus, teach me to pray. Amen.

LESSON TWENTY-NINE

Our Boldness in Prayer

> "And this is the confidence that we have in Him, that, if we *ask anything according to his will*, he heareth us. And if we know that he hear us, *whatsoever we ask*, we know that *we have the petitions* that we desired of him" (1 John 5:14, 15).

Undoubtedly, one of the greatest hindrances to believing prayer is this: many do not know if what they ask agrees with the will of God. As long as they are in doubt on this point, they cannot have the boldness to ask in the assurance that they certainly shall receive. And they soon begin to think that, if once they have made known their requests, and receive no answer, it is best to leave it to God to do according to His good pleasure. The words of John, "If we ask anything *according to his will*, he heareth us," as they understand them, make certainty as to answer to prayer impossible, because they cannot be sure of what really may be the will of God. They think of God's will as His hidden counsel. How should man be able to fathom what really may be the purpose of the all-wise God?

This is the very opposite of what John aimed at in writing about this. He wished to arouse us to boldness, to confidence, to full assurance of faith in prayer. He says, *"This is the boldness which we have toward him,"* that we can say: "Father, You know and I know that I ask according to your will. I know you hear me." "This is the boldness, that if we ask anything according to his will, he heareth us." But He adds at once: "If we know that he heareth us whatsoever we ask, we *know*," through this faith, "that we have," that we now while we pray receive "the petition," the special things, we have asked of Him.

John supposes that when we pray, we first find out if our prayers are according to the will of God. They may be according to God's will, and yet not come at once, or without the persevering prayer of faith. To encourage us to persevere and be strong in faith, He tells us that if we ask anything according to His will, He hears us. It is evident that if we are uncertain whether our petitions are according to His will, we cannot have the comfort of what he says, "We know that we have the petitions which we have asked of him."

But just this is the difficulty. More than one believer says: "I do not know if what I desire is according to the will of God. God's will is the purpose of His infinite wisdom. It is impossible for me to know whether He may not count something else better for me than what I desire, or may have some reasons for withholding what I ask." Everyone feels how with such thoughts, the prayer of faith described by Jesus, "Whosoever shall believe that *these things which he saith* shall come to pass, he shall have *whatsoever* he saith," becomes an impossibility. There may be the prayer of submission and of trust in God's wisdom, but there cannot be the prayer of faith. The great mistake here is that God's children do not really believe that it is possible to know God's will. Or if they believe this, they do not take the time and trouble to find it out. What we need is to see clearly how the Father leads His waiting, teachable child to know that his petition is according to His will.[1] We shall learn to know that our petitions are according to His will through God's holy Word received into the heart, life and will, and through God's Holy Spirit, accepted in His indwelling and leading.

There is a secret will of God with which we often fear that our prayers may be at odds. It is not with this will of God, but His will as revealed in His Word, that we are dealing with in prayer. Our notions of what the secret will may have decreed, and of how it might render the answers to our prayers impossible, are mostly erroneous. Childlike faith as to what He is willing to do for His children simply believes the Father's assurance that it is His will to hear prayer and to do what faith in His Word desires and accepts.

In the Word, the Father has revealed in general promises the great principles of His will with His people. The child has to take the promise and apply it to the special circumstances in his life to which it has reference. Whatever he asks within the limits of that revealed will, he can know to be according to the will of God, and he may confidently expect. In His Word, God has given us the revelation of His will and plans for us, for His people, and for the world. Also He gives the most precious promises of the grace and power with which He will carry out His plans and do His work through His people.

As faith becomes strong and bold enough to claim the fulfillment of the general promise in the special case, we may have the assurance that our prayers are heard. They are according to God's will. Take the words of John in the verse following our text as an illustration: "If any man see his brother sinning a sin not unto death, he shall ask and *God will give him life*." Such is the general promise; and the believer who pleads on the ground of this promise prays according to the will of God, and John would give him boldness to know that he has the petition which he asks.

But this comprehension of God's will is something spiritual, and must be spiritually discerned. It is not as a matter of logic that we can argue it out. God has said it; I must have it. Nor has every Christian the same gift or calling. While the general will revealed in the promise is the same for all, there is for each one a different special will according to God's purpose. Herein is the wisdom of the saints, to know this special will of God for each of us according to the measure of grace given us. Then we ask in prayer just what God has prepared and made possible for each. It is to communicate this wisdom *that the Holy Spirit dwells in us*. Then the Holy Spirit is given to us to lead us to the personal application of the general promises of the Word to our special personal needs.

This union of the teaching of the Word and Spirit many do

not understand, and so there is a twofold difficulty in knowing what God's will may be. Some seek the will of God in an inner feeling or conviction and want the Spirit to lead them without the Word. Others seek it in the Word without the living leading of the Holy Spirit. The two must be united: only in the Word, only in the Spirit, but in these assuredly, we can know the will of God and learn to pray according to it.

In the heart the Word and Spirit must meet. Only by their indwelling can we experience their teaching. The Word must dwell, must abide in us. Heart and life must day by day be under its influence. Not from without, but from within, comes the quickening of the Word by the Spirit. Only he who yields himself entirely in his whole life to the supremacy of the Word and the will of God can expect to discern what that word is and permit him boldly to ask in special cases. With the Spirit, just as with the Word, if I would have His leading in prayer to assure me what God's will is, my whole life must be yielded to that leading. Only that way can mind and heart become spiritual and capable of knowing God's holy will. He who, through word and Spirit, *lives in the will* of God by doing it, will know to pray according to that will in the confidence that He hears us.

Would that Christians might see what incalculable harm they do themselves by the thought that because possibly their prayer is not according to God's will, they must be content without an answer. God's Word tells us that the great reason of unanswered prayer is that we do not pray in the right way. "Ye ask and receive not, because ye ask amiss." In not granting an answer, the Father tells us that there is something wrong in our praying. He wants to teach us to find out and confess the problem and so educate us to true believing and prevailing prayer. He can attain His object only when He brings us to see that we are to blame for the withholding of the answer. Our aim or our faith or our life are not what they should be. But this purpose of God is frustrated as long as we are content to say: "Perhaps because my prayer is not according to His will, He does not hear me."

Let us no longer throw the blame of our unanswered prayers on the secret will of God, but on our own praying amiss. Let that word, "Ye receive not, because ye ask amiss," be as the lantern of the Lord, searching heart and life to prove that we are indeed just like those to whom Christ gave His promises of certain answers. Let us believe that we *can know* if our prayer be according to God's will. Let us yield our heart to have the word of the Father dwell richly there, to have Christ's word abiding in us. Let us live day by day with the anointing which teaches all things. Let us yield ourselves unreservedly to the Holy Spirit as He teaches us to abide in Christ and to dwell in the Father's presence. We shall soon understand how the Father's love longs that the child should know His will, and should, in the confidence that that will includes all that His power and love have promised to do, know too that He hears the petitions which we ask of Him. "*This is* the boldness which we have, that if we ask anything according to his will, he heareth us."

Blessed Master, with my whole heart I thank you for this wonderful lesson, that the path to a life full of answers to prayer is through the will of God. Lord, teach me to know this blessed will by living it, loving it, and always doing it. So shall I learn to offer prayers according to that will, and to find in harmony with God's blessed will my boldness in prayer and my confidence in accepting the answer.

Father, it is your will that your child should enjoy your presence and blessing. It is your will that everything in the life of your child should be in accordance with your will, and that the Holy Spirit should work this in him. It is your will that your child should live in the daily experience of distinct answers to prayer, so as to enjoy living and direct fellowship with you. It is your will that your name should be glorified in and through your children, and that it will be in those who trust you. Father, let your will be my confidence in all I ask.

Blessed Saviour, teach me to believe in the glory of this will. That will is the eternal love, which with divine power works out its purpose in each human will that yields itself to it. Lord, teach me this. You can make me see how every promise and every command of the Word is indeed the will of God, and that its fulfillment is sure for me because God himself guarantees it. Let the will of God become to me the rock on which my prayer and my assurance of an answer ever rest. Amen.

NOTE

There is often great confusion as to the will of God. People think that what God wills must inevitably take place. This is by no means the case. God wills a great deal of blessing to His people, which never comes to them. He wills it most earnestly, but they do not will it, and it cannot come to them. This is the great mystery of man's creation with a free will, and also of the renewal of his will in redemption, that God has made the execution of His will, in many things, dependent on the will of man. Of God's will revealed in His promises, as much will be fulfilled as our faith accepts. Prayer is the power by which that comes to pass which otherwise would not take place. <u>Faith is the power by which it is decided how much of God's will shall be done in us</u>. When once God reveals to a soul what He is willing to do for it, the responsibility for the execution of that will rests with us.

Some are afraid that this is putting too much power into the hands of man. But all power is put into the hands of man in Christ Jesus. The key of all prayer and all power is His. When we learn to understand that He is just as much one with us as with the Father, and that we are also just as much one with Him as He with the Father, we shall see how natural and right and safe it is that to those who abide in Him as He in the Father such power should be given. It is Christ the Son who has the right to ask what He will: it is through the abiding in Him and His abiding in us (in a divine reality of which we have too little understanding) that His Spirit breathes in us what He wants to ask and obtain through us. We pray in His name: the prayers are really ours and just as truly His.

Again others fear that to believe that prayer has such power is limiting the liberty and the love of God. If we only knew how we are limiting His liberty and His love by not allowing Him to act in the only way in which He chooses to act, now that He has taken us up into fellowship with himself—through our prayers and our faith. As we were speaking on this subject a brother in the ministry once asked whether there was not a danger of our thinking that our love for souls and our willingness to see them blessed were to move God's love and God's willingness to bless them. We were just passing some large waterpipes, which carried water over hill and dale from a large mountain stream to a town at some distance. Just look at these pipes, was the answer; they did not make the water willing to flow downwards from the hills, nor did they give it its power of blessing and refreshment. This is its very nature. All that they could do is to decide its direction. By it the inhabitants of the town said they want the blessing there. Just so, it is the very nature of God to love and to bless. Downward and ever downward His love longs to come with its quickening and refreshing streams. But He has left it to prayer to specify where the blessing is to come. He has committed it to His believing people to bring the living water to the desert places. The will of God to bless is dependent upon the will of man to say where the blessing must descend. "Such honor have all his saints." "And this is *the boldness* which we have toward him, that if we ask anything according to his will, he heareth us. And if *we know* that he hear us, whatsoever we ask, *we know that we have* the petitions which we have asked of him."

---

[1]See this illustrated in the extracts from George Muller at the end of this volume.

The Ministry of Intercession

" . . . an holy priesthood, to offer up spiritual sacrifices, acceptable to God by Jesus Christ" (1 Pet. 2:5).
"Ye shall be named the priests of the Lord" (Isa. 61:6).

"The Spirit of the Lord God is upon me because the Lord hath anointed me." These are the words of Jesus in Isaiah. As the fruit of His work all redeemed ones are priests, fellow-partakers with Him of His anointing with the Spirit as High Priest. "Like the precious ointment upon the beard of Aaron, that went down to the skirts of his garments." As did every son of Aaron, so does every member of Jesus' body have a right to the priesthood. But not everyone exercises it. Many are still entirely ignorant of it. And yet it is the highest privilege and likeness to Him, "who ever liveth to pray." Do you doubt if this is really true? Think of what constitutes priesthood.

There is, first, the *work of the priesthood.* This has two sides: Godward and manward. "Every priest is *ordained for men* in things *pertaining to God*" (Heb. 5:1); or as it is said by Moses (Deut. 10:8; see also 21:5; 33:10; Mal. 2:6): "The Lord separated the tribe of Levi, *to stand before the Lord* to minister unto him, and *bless his name.*" On the one hand the priest had the power to draw near to God, to dwell with Him in His house, and to present

175

before Him the blood of the sacrifice or the burning incense. This work he did not do on his own behalf, however, but for the sake of the people whose representative he was. This is the other side of his work. He received from the people their sacrifices, presented them before God, and then came out to bless in His name, to give the assurance of His favor and to teach them His law.

So a priest is a man who does not live at all for himself. *He lives with God and for God.* His work is as God's servant to care for His house, His honor, and His worship, to make known to men His love and His will. *He lives with men and for men* (Heb. 5:2). His work is to find out their sin and need and to bring it before God, to offer sacrifice and incense in their name, to obtain forgiveness and blessing for them, and then to come out and bless them in His name. This is the high calling of every believer. "Such honor have all his saints." They had been redeemed with the one purpose of being God's priests in the midst of the perishing millions around them. In conformity to Jesus, the Great High Priest, God's priests are to be the ministers and stewards of His grace to all around them.

And then there is *the walk of the priesthood,* in harmony with its work. As God is holy, so the priest was to be especially holy. This means not only separated from everything unclean, but *holy unto God,* being set apart and given up to God for His disposal. The separation from the world and setting apart unto God was indicated in many ways.

It was seen in the clothing: the holy garments, made after God's own order, marked them as His (Ex. 28). It was seen in the command as to their special purity and freedom from all contact from death and defilement (Lev. 21:22). Much that was allowed to an ordinary Israelite was forbidden to them. It was seen in the injunction that the priest must have no bodily defect or blemish; bodily perfection was to be the type of wholeness and holiness in God's service. And it was seen in the arrangement by which the priestly tribes were to have no inheritance with the other tribes; God was to be their inheritance. Their life was to be one of faith; set apart unto God, they were to live in Him as well as for Him.

All this is the emblem of what the character of the New Testament priest is to be. Our priestly power with God depends on our personal life and walk. We must be of those of whose walk on earth Jesus says, "They have not defiled their garments."

In the surrender of what may appear lawful to others in our separation from the world, we must prove that our consecration to be holy to the Lord is wholehearted and complete. The bodily perfection of the priest must have its counterpart in our too being "without spot or blemish"; "the man of God perfect, throughly furnished unto all good works," "perfect and entire, wanting nothing" (Lev. 21:17-21; Eph. 5:27; 2 Tim. 2:7; Jas. 1:4). Above all, we consent to give up all inheritance on earth, to forsake all, and like Christ to have only God as our portion. To possess as not possessing and hold all for God alone marks the true priest, the man who only lives for God and his fellowmen.

And now, *the way to the priesthood*. In Aaron God had chosen all his sons to be priest. Each of them was a priest by birth. But he could not enter upon his work without a special act of ordinance—his consecration. Every child of God is priest in right of his birth, his blood relationship to the Great High Priest. But this is not enough—he will exercise his power only as he accepts and realizes his consecration.

With Aaron and his sons it took place this way (Ex. 29): After being washed and clothed, they were anointed with the holy oil. Sacrifices were then offered. Then with the blood the right ear, the right hand, and the right foot were touched. And then they and their garments were once again sprinkled with the blood and the oil together. As the child of God understands more fully what the blood and the Spirit, of which he already is partaker, are to him, the power of the Holy Priesthood will work in him. The blood will take away all sense of unworthiness; the Spirit, all sense of unfitness.

Let us notice what there was new in the application of the blood to the priest. If ever he had as a penitent brought a sacrifice for his sin, seeking forgiveness, the blood was sprinkled on the altar but not on his person. Now, for priestly consecration there was to be closer contact with the blood. Ear and hand and foot were by a special act brought under its power, and the whole being taken possession of and sanctified for God. So, when the believer, who had been content to think chiefly of the blood sprinkled on the mercy seat as what he needs for pardon, is led to seek full priestly access to God, he feels the need of a fuller and more abiding experience of the power of the blood. He needs a true sprinkling and cleansing of the heart from an evil conscience, so that he has "no more conscience of sin" (Heb. 10:2). And it is as he gets to enjoy this that the consciousness is awakened of his wonderful right of most intimate access to God and of the full assurance that his intercessions are acceptable.

And as the blood gives the right, the Spirit gives the power, and equips us for believing intercession. He breathes into us the priestly spirit—burning love for God's honor and the saving of souls. He makes us so one with Jesus that prayer in His name is a reality. He strengthens us to believing, importunate prayer. The more the Christian is truly filled with the Spirit of Christ, the more spontaneous will be his giving himself up to the life of priestly intercession. Beloved fellow Christians, God greatly needs priests who can draw near to Him, who live in His presence, and by their intercession bring down the blessing of His grace on others. And the world greatly needs priests who will bear the burden of the perishing ones and intercede on their behalf.

Are you willing to offer yourself for this holy work? You know the surrender it demands—nothing less than the Christlike giving up of all, so that the saving purposes of God's love may be accomplished among men. Be no longer one with those who are content if they have salvation and just do work enough to keep themselves warm and lively. Let nothing keep you back from giving yourselves to be wholly and only priests of the Most High God. The thought of unworthiness, of unfitness, need not keep you back. In *the blood*, the objective power of the perfect redemption works in you. In *the Spirit*, its full subjective personal experience as a divine life is secured. *The blood* provides an infinite worthiness to make your prayers most acceptable. *The Spirit* provides a divine fitness, teaching you to pray according to the will of God. *Every priest knew that when he presented a sacrifice according to the law of the sanctuary, it was accepted.* Under the covering of the blood and Spirit, you have the assurance that all the wonderful promises to prayer in the name Jesus will be fulfilled in you. Abiding in union with the Great High Priest, "you shall ask what you will, and it shall be done unto you." You will have power to pray the effectual prayer of the righteous man that avails much. You will not only join in the general prayer of the Church for the world, but be able in your own sphere to take up your special work in prayer—as priests, to transact it with God, to receive and know the answer, and so to bless in His name. Come and be a priest, *only* priest, *all* priest. Seek to walk before the Lord in the full consciousness that you have been set apart for the holy ministry of intercession. This is the true blessedness of conformity to the image of God's Son.

My blessed High Priest, accept the consecration in which my soul now would respond to your message.

I believe in the holy priesthood of your saints, I believe that I too am a priest, with power to appear before the Father, and in the prayer that avails much to bring down blessing on the perishing around me.

I believe in the power of your precious blood to cleanse me from all sin, to give me perfect confidence toward God, and bring me near in the full assurance of faith that my intercession will be heard.

I believe in the anointing of the Spirit, coming down daily from you, my Great High Priest, to sanctify me, to fill me with the consciousness of my priestly calling, and with love for souls, to teach me what is according to God's will, and how to pray the prayer of faith.

I believe that, as you, my Lord Jesus, are yourself in all things my life, so you, too, are the surety for my prayer life. You will include me in the fellowship of your wondrous work of intercession.

In this faith, I yield myself this day to my God, as one of His anointed priest, to stand before His face to intercede in behalf of sinners, and to come out and bless in His name.

Holy Lord Jesus, accept and seal my consecration. Lord, lay your hands on me, and consecrate me to this holy work. Let me walk among men with the consciousness and the character of a priest of the Most High God.

"Unto him that loved us, and washed us from our sins in his own blood, and hath made us kings and priest unto God and his Father; to him be glory and dominion for ever and ever. Amen.

A Life of Prayer

"Rejoice evermore. Pray without ceasing. In everything give thanks" (1 Thess. 5:16-18).

Our Lord gave the parable of the widow and the unjust judge to teach us that men ought to always pray and not faint. As the widow persevered in seeking one definite thing, the parable seems to refer to persevering prayer for some one blessing, when God delays or appears to refuse. The words in the Epistles, which speak of continuing instant in prayer, continuing in prayer and watching in the same, of praying always in the Spirit, appear to refer more to the whole life being one of prayer. As the soul fills with longing for the manifestation of God's glory to us and in us, through us and around us, and with the confidence that He hears the prayers of His children, the inmost life of the soul is continually rising upward in dependence and faith, in longing desire and trustful expectation.

What is needed to live such a life of prayer? The first thing is undoubtedly the entire sacrifice of the life to God's kingdom and glory. He who seeks to pray without ceasing because he wants to be very pious and good will never attain to it. It is by forgetting self and yielding ourselves to live for God and His honor that the heart is enlarged and teaches us to regard everything in the light of God and His will. It is the instinctive recognition that everything around us needs God's help and blessing; all is opportunity for His being glorified. Because everything is weighed and tested by the one thing that fills the heart—the glory of God—and because the soul has learned that only what is of God can really be for Him and His glory, the whole life becomes a looking up, a crying from the inmost heart, for God to prove His power and love, and so show forth His glory. The believer awakens to the consciousness that he is one of the watchman on Zion's walls, one of the Lord's remembrancers, whose call really does touch and move the King in heaven to do what would otherwise not be done. He understands how real Paul's exhortation was, "praying always with all prayer and supplication in the Spirit for all the saints and for me," and "continue in prayer, withal praying also for us." To forget oneself, to live for God and His kingdom among men, is the way to learn to pray without ceasing.

This life devoted to God must be accompanied by the deep confidence that our prayer is effective. In His prayer-lessons our Blessed Lord insisted upon nothing so much as faith in God as a Father who most certainly does what we ask. "Ask and ye shall receive"; to count confidently on an answer is with Him the beginning and the end of His teaching (compare Matt. 7:8 and John 16:24). In proportion as this assurance masters us, and it becomes a settled thing that our prayers do tell and that God does what we ask, we dare not neglect the use of this wonderful power. The soul turns wholly to God, and our life becomes prayer. We see that the Lord needs and takes time, because we and all around us are the creatures of time, under the law of growth. Knowing that not one single prayer of faith can possibly be lost, that there is sometimes a need for the storing up and accumulating of prayer, but recognizing that persevering prayer is irresistible, prayer becomes the quiet, persistent living of our life of desire and faith in the presence of our God.

Let us no longer by our reasonings limit and enfeeble such free and sure promises of the living God, robbing them of their power, and ourselves of the wonderful confidence they are meant to inspire. Not in God, not in His secret will, not in the limitations of His promises, but in us is the hindrance. We are not what we should be to obtain the promise. Let us open our whole heart to God's words of promise in all their simplicity and truth. They will search us and humble us. They will lift us up and makes us glad and strong. To the faith that knows it gets what it asks, prayer is not work or a burden, but a joy and a triumph. It becomes a necessity and a second nature.

This union of strong desire and firm confidence again is nothing but the life of the Holy Spirit within us. The Holy Spirit dwells in us, hides himself in the depths of our being, and stirs the desire after the unseen and the divine, after God himself. Whether groanings that cannot be uttered, or in clear and conscious assurance; whether in special petitions for the deeper revelation of Christ to us, or in pleadings for a soul, a work, the Church or the world, it is always and alone the work of the Holy Spirit. He draws out the heart to thirst for God, to long for His being made known and glorified.

Where the child of God really lives and walks in the Spirit, where he is not content to remain carnal, but seeks to be spiritual, in everything a fit organ for the divine Spirit to reveal the life of Christ and Christ himself, there the never-ceasing intercession life of the Blessed Son is revealed and then repeats itself in our experience. Because it is the Spirit of Christ who prays in us, our prayer must be heard; because it is we who pray in the Spirit, there is need of time, and patience, and continual renewing of the prayer until every obstacle be conquered and the harmony between God's Spirit and ours is perfect.

But the most important thing we need for such a life of unceasing prayer is to know that Jesus teaches us to pray. We have begun to understand a little what *His* teaching is. Not the communication of new thoughts or views, not the discovery of failure or error, not the stirring up of desire and faith, of however much importance all this be, but receiving us into the fellowship of His own prayer life before the Father—it is that by which Jesus really teaches.

It was the sight of the praying Jesus that aroused a desire, that made the disciples long and ask to be taught to pray. It is the faith of the ever-praying Jesus, to whom belongs the power to pray, that teaches us truly to pray. We know why: He who prays is our Head and our Life. All He has is ours and is given to us when we give ourselves all to Him. By His blood He leads us into the immediate presence of God. The inner sanctuary is our home; we dwell there. He that lives so near God, and knows that He has been brought near to bless those who are far, cannot help but pray. Christ makes us partakers with himself of His prayer power and prayer life. We understand then that our true aim must not be to work much, and have prayer enough to keep the work right, but to pray much and then to work enough for the power and blessing obtained in prayer to find its way through us to men. It is Christ who ever lives to pray, who saves and reigns. He communicates His prayer life to us. He maintains it in us if we trust Him. He is surety for our praying without ceasing. Christ teaches us to pray by showing how He does it, by doing it in us, by leading us to do it in Him and like Him. Christ is all, the life and the strength too for a never-ceasing prayer life.

The sight of this ever-praying Christ as our life enables us to pray without ceasing. Because His priesthood is the power of an endless life, that resurrection life that never fades and never fails, and because His life is our life, praying without ceasing can become to us nothing less than the joy of heaven. So the apostle says: "Rejoice *evermore:* pray *without ceasing; in everything* give thanks." Borne up between the never-ceasing joy and the never-ceasing praise, never-ceasing prayer is the manifestation of the power of the eternal life where Jesus always prays. The union between the Vine and the branch is indeed a prayer union. The highest conformity to Christ, the most blessed participation in the glory of His heavenly life is that we take part in His work of intercession. He and we ever live to pray. In the experience of our union with Him, praying without ceasing becomes not only a possibility, but also a reality, the holiest and most blessed part of our holy and blessed fellowship with God. We have our abode within the veil in the presence of the Father. What the Father says, we do; what the Son says, the Father does. Praying without ceasing is the earthly manifestation of heaven come down to us, the foretaste of the life where they rest not day or night in the song of worship and adoration.

Father, with my whole heart I praise you for this wondrous life of never-ceasing prayer, never-ceasing fellowship, never-ceasing answers, and never-ceasing experience of my oneness with Him who ever lives to pray. God, help me to dwell and walk in the presence of your glory always so that prayer may be the spontaneous expression of my life with you.

Blessed Saviour, with my whole heart I praise you that you came from heaven to share with me in my needs and cries, that I might share with you in your all-prevailing intercession. And I thank you that you have taken me into the school of prayer, to teach the blessedness and the power of a life that is all prayer. Thank you most of all, that you have taken me up into the fellowship of your life of intercession that through me too your blessings may be dispensed to those around me.

Holy Spirit, with deep reverence I thank you for your work in me. Through you I am allowed to share in the intimate relationship between the Son and the Father, and enter so into the fellowship of the life and love of the Holy Trinity. Spirit of God, perfect your work in me; bring me into perfect union with Christ my Intercessor. Let your unceasing indwelling make my life one of unceasing intercession. And so let my life become one that is unceasingly to the glory of the Father and to the blessing of those around me. Amen.

George Muller, and the Secret of His Power in Prayer

When God wishes to remind His Church of a truth that is not being understood or practiced, He usually does so by raising some man to be in word and deed a living witness to its blessedness. God therefore raised up in the nineteenth century, among others, George Muller to demonstrate that He is indeed the Hearer of prayer. I know of no way in which the principal truths of God's Word in regard to prayer can be more effectively illustrated and established than a short review of his life and of what he tells of his prayer-experiences.

Muller was born in Prussia on September 25, 1805 and died on March 10, 1898, at the age of 92. His early life, even after having entered the University of Halle as a theological student, was wicked in the extreme. When twenty years old, he was led by a friend one evening to a prayer meeting. He was deeply impressed, and soon after came to know the Saviour. Not long after, he began reading missionary papers, and in course of time offered himself to the London Society for promoting Christianity to the Jews. He was accepted as a student, but soon found that he could not in all things submit to the rules of the Society, as leaving too little liberty for the leading of the Holy Spirit. The connection was dissolved in 1830 by mutual consent, and he became the pastor of a small congregation at Teignmouth. In 1832, he was led to Bristol. There as pastor of Bethesda Chapel, he was led to the Orphan Home and other work, in connection with which God has so remarkably led him to trust His Word and to experience how God fulfills that Word.

A few quotations in regard to his spiritual life will prepare the way for what we especially wish to quote of his experiences in reference to prayer:

"In connection with this I would mention, that the Lord very graciously gave me, from the very commencement of my divine life, a measure of simplicity and of childlike disposition in spiritual things, so that whilst I was exceedingly ignorant of the Scriptures, and was still from time to time overcome even by outward sins, yet I was enabled to carry most minute matters to the *Lord in prayer.* And I have found 'godliness profitable unto all things, having promise of the life that now is, and of that which is to come.' Though very weak and ignorant, yet I had now, by the grace of God, some desire to benefit others, and he who so faithfully had once served Satan, sought now to win souls for Christ."

At Teignmouth he was led to know how to use God's Word, and to trust the Holy Spirit as the Teacher given by God to make that Word clear. He writes:

"God then began to show me that the Word of God alone is our standard of judgment in spiritual things; that it can be explained only by the Holy Spirit; and that in our day, as well as in former times, He is the Teacher of His people. The office of the Holy Spirit I had not experimentally understood before that time.

"It was my beginning to understand this latter point in particular, which had a great effect on me; for the Lord enabled me to put it to the test of experience, by laying aside commentaries, and almost every other book, and simply reading the Word of God and studying it.

"The result was that the first evening that I shut myself in my room, to give myself to prayer and meditation over the Scriptures, I learned more in a few hours than I had done during a period of several months previously.

"But the particular difference was that I received real strength for my soul in so doing. I now began to try by the test of the Scriptures the things which I had learned and seen, and found that only those principles which stood the test were of real value."

Of obedience to the Word of God, he writes in connection with his being baptized:

"It had pleased God, in His abundant mercy, to bring my mind into such a state that I was willing to carry out in my life whatever I should find in the Scriptures. I could say, 'I will do His will,' and it was on that account, I believe, that I saw which *'doctrine is of God.'* And I would observe here, by the way, that the passage to which I have just alluded (John 7:17) has been a most remarkable comment to me on many doctrines and precepts of our most holy faith. For instance; 'Resist not evil; but whosoever shall smite thee on thy right cheek, turn to him the other also. And if any man will sue thee at the law, and take away thy coat, let him have thy cloak also. And whosoever shall compel thee to go a mile, go with him twain. Give to him that asketh thee, and from him that would borrow of thee, turn not thou away. Love your enemies, bless them that curse you, do good to them that hate you, and pray for them which despitefully use you, and persecute you' (Matt. 5:39-44). 'Sell that ye have, and give alms' (Luke 12:33). 'Owe no man anything, but to love one another' (Rom. 13:8). It may be said, 'Surely these passages cannot be taken literally, for how then would the people of God be able to pass through the world?' The state of mind enjoined in John 7:17 will cause such objections to vanish. *Whosoever is willing to act out* these commandments of the Lord *literally,* will, I believe, be led with me to see that to take them *literally* is the will of God. Those who do *so* take them will doubtless often be brought into difficulties, hard to the flesh to bear, but these will have a tendency to make them constantly feel that they are strangers and pilgrims here, that this world is not their home, and thus to throw them more upon God, who will assuredly help us through any difficulty into which we may be brought by seeking to act in obedience to His Word."

This implicit surrender to God's Word led him to certain views and conduct in regard to money, which profoundly influenced his future life. They had their root in the conviction that money was a divine stewardship, and that all money had therefore to be received and dispensed in direct fellowship with God himself. This led him to the adoption of the following four great rules:

1. *Not to receive any fixed salary,* both because in the collecting of it there was often much that was at variance with the free-will offering with which God's service is to be maintained, and in the receiving of it a danger of placing more dependence on human sources of income than in the living God himself.

2. *Never to ask any human being for help,* however great the need might be, but to make his wants known to God who has promised to care for His servants and to hear their prayer.

3. *To take this command* (Luke 12:33) literally, *"Sell that thou hast and give alms,"* and never to save up money, but to spend all God entrusted to him on God's poor, on the work of His kingdom.

4. *Also to take Romans 13:8, "Owe no man anything," literally,* and never to buy on credit, or be in debt for anything, but to trust God to provide.

This mode of living was not easy at first. But Muller testifies it was most blessed in bringing the soul to rest in God, and drawing it into closer union with himself when inclined to backslide. *"For it will not do, it is not possible, to live in sin, and at the same time, by communion with God, to draw from heaven everything one needs for the life that now is."*

Not long after his settlement at Bristol, The Scriptural Knowledge Institution for Home and Abroad was established for aiding in day school, Sunday school, mission and Bible work. Of this institution the orphan home work, by which Mr. Muller is best known, became a branch. In 1834 his heart was touched by the case of an orphan brought to Christ in one of the schools, but who had to go to a poorhouse where his spiritual wants would not be cared for. Shortly after he writes (Nov. 20, 1835): "Today I have had it very much laid on my heart no longer merely to *think* about the establishment of an orphan home, but actually to set about it, and I have been very much in prayer respecting it, in order to ascertain the Lord's mind. May God make it plain." And again, Nov. 25: "I have been again much in prayer yesterday and today about the orphan home, and am more and more convinced that it is of God. May He in mercy guide me. The three chief reasons are: 1.) That God may be glorified, should He be pleased to furnish me with the means, in its being seen that it is not a vain thing to trust Him; and that thus the faith of His children may be strengthened. 2.) The spiritual welfare of fatherless and motherless children. 3.) Their temporal welfare."

After some months of prayer and waiting on God a house was rented, with room for thirty children, and in course of time three more, with room for 120 children. The work was carried on in this way for ten years, the supplies for the needs of the orphans being asked and received of God alone. It was often a time of sore need and much prayer, but a trial of faith more precious than of gold was found unto praise and honor and glory of God. The Lord was preparing His servant for greater things. By God's providence and His Holy Spirit, Mr. Muller was led to desire, and to wait upon God till he received from Him, the sure promise of £15,000 for a home to contain 300 children. This first home was opened in 1849. In 1858, a second and third home, for 950 more orphans, was opened, costing £35,000. And in 1869 and 1870, a fourth and a fifth home, for 850 more, at an expense of £50,000, making the total number of the orphans 2,100.

In addition to this work, God has given him almost as much money for other work—the support of schools and missions, and Bible tract circulation. In all he received from God, to be spent in His work, more than one million pounds sterling. How little he knew, let us carefully notice, that when he gave up his little salary of £30 a year in obedience to the leading of God's Word and Holy Spirit, what God was preparing to give him as the reward of obedience and faith; and how wonderfully the Word was to be fulfilled to him: "Thou hast been faithful over few things; I will set thee over many things."

And these things have happened for an examaple to us. God calls us to be followers of George Muller, even as he was of Christ. His God is our God; the same promises are for us; the same service of love and faith in which he labored is called for us on every side. Let us study the way in which God gave George Muller such power as a man of prayer; we shall find in it the most remarkable illustration of some of the lessons which we have been studying with the blessed Master in the Word. We shall especially have impressed upon us His first great lesson, that if we will come to Him in the way He has pointed out, with definite petitions, made known to us by the Spirit through the Word as being according to the will of God, we may confidently believe that whatsoever we ask shall be done.

PRAYER AND THE WORD OF GOD

We have repeatedly seen that God's listening to our voice depends upon our listening to His voice. (See Lessons 22 and 23.) We must not only have a special promise to plead, when we make a special request, but our whole life must be under the supremacy of the Word—the Word must be dwelling in us. The testimony of George Muller on this point is most instructive. He tells us how the discovery of the true place of the Word of God, and the teaching of the Spirit with it, was the commencement of a new era in his spiritual life. Of it he writes:

"Now the scriptural way of reasoning would have been: God himself has condescended to become an author, and I am ignorant about that precious book which His Holy Spirit has caused to be written through the instrumentality of His servants, and it contains that which I ought to know, and the knowledge of which will lead me to true happiness; therefore I ought to read again and again this most precious book, this book of books, most earnestly, most prayerfully, and with much mediation; and in this practice I ought to contiune all the days of my life. For I was aware, though I read it but little, that I knew scarcely anything of it. But instead of acting thus, and being led by my ignorance of the Word of God to study it more, my difficulty in understanding it, and the little enjoyment I had in it, made me careless of reading it (for much prayerful reading of the Word gives not merely more knowledge, but increases the delight we have in reading it); and thus, like many believers, I practically preferred, for the first four years of my divine life, the works of uninspired men to the oracles of the living God. The consequence was that I remained a babe, both in knowledge and grace. In knowledge, I say; for all *true* knowledge must be derived, by the Spirit, from the Word. And as I neglected the Word, I was for nearly four years so ignorant that I did not *clearly* know even the *fundamental* points of our holy faith. And this lack of knowledge most sadly kept me back from walking steadily in the ways of God. For when it pleased the Lord in August 1829 to bring me really to the Scriptures, my life and walk became very different. And though ever since that I have very much fallen short of what I might and ought to be, yet by the grace of God I have been enabled to live much nearer to Him than before. If any believers read this who practically prefer other books to the Holy Scriptures, and who enjoy the writings of men much more than the Word of God, may they be warned by my loss. I shall consider this book to have been the means of doing good, should it please the Lord, through its instrumentality, to lead some of His people no longer to neglect the Holy Scriptures, but to give them that preference which they have hitherto bestowed on the writings of men.

"Before I leave this subject, I would only add: If the reader understands very little of the Word of God, he ought to read it very much; for the Spirit explains the Word by the Word. And if he enjoys the reading of the Word little, that is just the reason why he should read it much; for the frequent reading of the Scriptures creates a delight in them, so that the more we read them, the more we desire to do so.

"Above all, he should seek to have it settled in his own mind that God alone by His Spirit can teach him, and that therefore, as God will be inquired of for blessings, it becomes him to seek God's blessing previous to reading, and also whilst reading.

"He should have it, moreover, settled in his mind that although the Holy Spirit is the *best* and *sufficient* Teacher, yet that his Teacher does not always teach immediately *when* we desire it, and that therefore, we may have to entreat Him again and again for the explanation of certain passages; but that He will surely teach us at last, if indeed we are seeking for light prayerfully, patiently, and with a view to the glory of God."[1]

We find in his journal frequent mention made of two and three hours spent in prayer over the Word for the feeding of his spiritual life. As the fruit of this, when he had need of strength and encouragement in prayer, the individual promises were not to him so many arguments from a book to be used with God. They were instead living words which he had heard the Father's living voice speak to him, and which he could now bring to the Father in living faith.

PRAYER AND THE WILL OF GOD

One of young believers' greatest difficulties is to know how they can find out whether what they desire is according to God's will. One of the most precious lessons God wants to teach through the experience of George Muller is that He is willing to make known things of which His Word says nothing directly, that they are His will for us, and that we may ask them. The teaching of the Spirit (not without or against the Word) as something above, beyond and in addition to it, without which we cannot see God's will, is the heritage of every believer. It is through *the Word, and the Word alone,* that the Spirit teaches, applying the general principles or promises to our special need. And it is *the Spirit, and the Spirit alone,* who can really make the Word a light on our path, whether the path of duty in our daily walk, or the path of faith in our approach to God. Let us notice in what childlike simplicity and teachableness it was that the discovery of God's will was so surely and so clearly made known to Mr. Muller.

With regard to the building of the first home and the assurance he had of its being God's will, he wrote in May 1850, just after it had been opened. Speaking of the great difficulties there were, and how unlikely it appeared to nature that they would be removed, "But while the prospect before me would have been overwhelming had I looked at it naturally, I was never even for once permitted to question how it would end. For as from the beginning I was sure *it was the will of God* that I should go to the work of building for Him this large Orphan Home, so also from the beginning I was a certain that the whole would be finished as if the home had been already filled."

The way in which he found out what was God's will comes out with special clarity in his account of the building of the second home. Study with care the lesson the narrative conveys:

December 5, 1850.—"Under these circumstances I can only pray that the Lord in His tender mercy would not allow Satan to gain an advantage over me. By the grace of God my heart says: Lord, if I could be sure that it is Thy will that I should go forward in this matter, I would do so cheerfully; and, on the other hand, if I could be sure that these are vain, foolish, proud thoughts, that they are not from Thee, I would, by Thy grace, hate them, and entirely put them aside.

"My hope is in God: He will help and teach me. Judging, however, from His former dealings with me, it would not be a strange thing to me, nor surprising, if He called me to labor yet still more largely in this way.

"The thoughts about enlarging the orphan work have not yet arisen on account of an abundance of money having lately come in; for I have had of late to wait for about seven weeks upon God, whilst little, very little comparatively, came in, *i.e.,* about four times as much was going out as came in; and, had not the Lord previously sent me large sums, we should have been distressed indeed.

"Lord! how can Thy servant know Thy will in this matter! Wilt Thou be pleased to teach him!

December 11.—"During the last six days, since writing the above, I have been, day after day, waiting upon God concerning this matter. It has generally been more or less all the day on my heart. When I have been awake at night, it has not been far from my thoughts. Yet all this without the least excitement. I am perfectly calm and quiet respecting it. My soul would be rejoiced to go forward in this service could I be sure that the Lord would have me to do so; for then, notwithstanding the numberless difficulties, all would be well; and His Name would be magnified.

"On the other hand, were I assured that the Lord would have me to be satisfied with my present sphere of service, and that I should not pray about enlarging the work, by His grace I should not pray about enlarging the work, by His grace I could, *without any effort,* cheerfully yield to it; for He has brought me into such a state of heart that I only desire to please Him in this matter. Moreover, hitherto I have not spoken about this thing even to my beloved wife, the sharer of my joys, sorrows, and labors for more than twenty years; nor is it likely that I shall do so for some time to come: for I prefer quietly to wait on the Lord, without conversing on this subject, in order that thus I may be kept the more easily, by His blessing, from being influenced by things from without. The burden of my prayer concerning this matter is, that the Lord would not allow me to make a mistake, and that He would teach me to do His will.

December 26.—"Fifteen days have elapsed since I wrote the preceding paragraph. Every day since then I have continued to pray about this matter, and that with a goodly measure of earnestness, by the help of God. There has passed scarcely an hour during these days, in which, whilst awake, this matter has not been more or less before me. But all without even a shadow of excitement. I converse with no one about it. Hitherto have I not even done so with my dear wife. From this I refrain still, and deal with God alone about the matter, in order that no outward influence and no outward excitement may keep me from attaining unto *a clear discovery of His will. I have the fullest and most peaceful assurance that He will clearly show me His will.* This evening I have had again an especially solemn season of prayer, to seek to know the will of God. But whilst I continue to entreat and beseech the Lord that He would not allow me to be deluded in this business, I may say I have scarcely any doubt remaining on my mind as to what will be the issue, even that I should go forward in this matter. As this, however, is one of the most momentous steps that I have ever taken, I judge that I cannot go about this matter with too much caution, prayerfulness, and deliberation. I am in no hurry about it. I could wait for years, by God's grace, were this His will, before even taking one single step toward this thing, or even speaking to anyone about it; and, on the other hand, I would set to work tomorrow, were the Lord to bid me do so. This calmness of mind, this having no will of my own in the matter, this only wishing to please my Heavenly Father in it, this only seeking His and not my honor in it; this state of heart, I say, is the fullest assurance to me that my heart is not under a fleshly excitement, and that, if I am helped thus to go on, *I shall know the will of God to the full.* But, while I write this, I cannot but add at the same time, that I do crave the honor and the glorious privilege to be more and more used by the Lord.

"I desire to be allowed to provide scriptural instruction for a thousand orphans, instead of doing so for 300. I desire to expound the Holy Scriptures regularly to a thousand orphans, instead of doing so to 300. I desire that it may be yet more abundantly manifest that God is still the Hearer and Answerer of prayer, and that He is the living God now as He ever was and ever will be, when He shall simply, in answer to prayer, have condescended to provide me with a house for 700 orphans and with means to support them. This last consideration is the most important point in my mind. The Lord's honor is the principal point with me in this whole matter; and just because this is the case, if He would be more glorified by not going forward in this business, I should by His grace be perfectly content to give up all thoughts about another orphan house. Surely in such a state of mind, obtained by the Holy Spirit, Thou, O my Heavenly Father, *wilt not suffer Thy child to be mistaken, much less deluded.* By the help of God I shall continue further day by day to wait upon Him in prayer, concerning this thing, till He shall bid me act.

January 2, 1851.—"A week ago I wrote the preceding paragraph. During this week I have still been helped day by day, and more than once every day, to seek the guidance of the Lord about another orphan house. The burden of my prayer has still been, that He in His great mercy would keep me from making a mistake. During the last week the book of Proverbs has come in the course of my Scripture reading, and my heart has been refreshed in reference to this subject by the following passage: 'Trust in the Lord with all thine heart; and lean not unto thine own understanding. In all thy ways acknowledge him, and he shall direct thy paths' (Prov. 3:5, 6). By the grace of God I do acknowledge the Lord in all my ways, and in this thing in particular. I have therefore the comfortable assurance that He will direct my paths concerning this part of my service, as to whether I shall be occupied in it or not. Further: 'The integrity of the upright shall preserve them' (Prov. 11:3). By the grace of God I am upright in this business. My honest purpose is to get glory to God. Therefore I expect to be guided aright. Further: 'Commit thy works unto the Lord, and thy thoughts shall be established' (Prov. 16:3). I do commit my works unto the Lord, and therefore expect that my thoughts will be established. My heart is more and more coming to a calm, quiet, and settled assurance that the Lord will condescend to use me still further in the orphan work. Here, Lord, is Thy servant."

When later he decided to build two additional houses, Numbers 4 and 5, he writes as follows:

"Twelve days have passed since I wrote the last paragraph. I have still day by day been enabled to wait upon the Lord with reference to enlarging the orphan work, and have been during the whole of this period also in perfect peace, which is the result of seeking in this thing only the Lord's honor and the temporal and spiritual benefit of my fellowmen. Without an effort could I by His grace put aside all thoughts about this whole affair, if only assured that it is the will of God that I should do so; and, on the other hand, would at once go forward, if He would have it be so. I have still kept this matter entirely to myself. Though it be now about seven weeks, since day by day, more or less, my mind has been exercised about it, and since I have been daily praying about it, yet not one human being knows of it. As yet I have not even mentioned it to my dear wife, in order that thus, by quietly waiting upon God, I might not be influenced by what might be said to me on the subject. This evening has been particularly set apart for prayer, beseeching the Lord once more not to allow me to be mistaken in this thing, and much less to be deluded by the devil. I have also sought to let all the reasons *against* building another orphan house, and all the reasons *for* doing so pass before my mind: and now for the clearness and definiteness, write them down. . . .

"Much, however, as the nine previous reasons weigh with me, yet they would not decide me were there not one more. It is this. After having for months pondered the matter, and having looked at it in all its bearings and with all its difficulties, and then having been finally led, after much prayer, to decide on this enlargement, my mind is at peace. The child who has again and again besought His Heavenly Father not to allow him to be deluded, nor even to make a mistake, is at peace, perfectly at peace concerning this decision; and has thus the assurance that the decision come to, after much prayer during weeks and months, is the leading of the Holy Spirit; and therefore purposes to go forward, assuredly believing that he will not be confounded, for he trusts in God. Many and great may be his difficulties; thousands and ten thousands of prayers may have ascended to God before the full answer may be obtained; much exercise of faith and patience may be required; but in the end it will again be seen, that His servant, who trusts in Him, has not been confounded."

PRAYER AND THE GLORY OF GOD

We have sought more than once to emphasize this truth: we ordinarily seek the reasons of our prayers not being heard in whether or not we asked according to the will of God. Scripture warns us to find the cause in ourselves, in our not being in the right state or not asking in the right spirit. The thing may be in full accordance with His will, but the asking, the spirit of the one who asks, not; therefore we are not heard. As the great root of all sin is self and self-seeking, so there is nothing that in our more spiritual desires so effectually hinders God in answering as this: praying for our own pleasure or glory. Prayer, to have power and prevail, must ask for the glory of God; one can only pray thus as he is living for God's glory.

In George Muller we have one of the most remarkable instances on record of God's Holy Spirit leading a man deliberately and systematically, at the outset of a course of prayer, to make the glorifying of God his first and only object. Ponder well what he says, and learn the lesson God would teach us through him:

"I had constantly cases brought before me, which proved that one of the special things which the children of God needed in our day was *to have their faith strengthened.*

"I longed, therefore, to have something to point my brethren to, as a visible proof that our God and Father is the same faithful God as ever He was; as willing as ever to *prove* himself to be the living God in our day as formerly, *to all who put their trust in Him.*

"My spirit longed to be instrumental in strengthening their faith, by giving them not only instances from the Word of God, of His willingness and ability to help all who rely upon Him, but to *show them* by proofs that He is the same in our day. I knew that the Word of God ought to be enough, and it was by grace enough for me; but still I considered I ought to lend a helping hand to my brethren.

"I therefore judged myself bound to be the servant of the Church of Christ, in the particular point in which I had obtained mercy; namely, in being able to take God at His Word and rely upon it. The first object of the work was, and is still: *that God might be magnified* by the fact that the orphans under my care are provided with all they need, *only by prayer and faith,* without anyone being asked; thereby it may be seen that God is *faithful still, and hears prayer still.*

"When I began the orphan work in 1835, my chief object was the glory of God, by giving a practical demonstration as to what could be accomplished simply through the instrumentality of prayer and faith, in order thus to benefit the Church at large, and to lead a careless world to see the reality of the things of God, by showing them in this work, that the living God is still, as 4000 years ago, the living God. This my aim has been abundantly honored. Multitudes of sinners have been thus converted, multitudes of the children of God in all parts of the world have been benefited by this work, even as I had anticipated. But the larger the work has grown, the greater has been the blessing, bestowed in the very way in which I looked for blessing: for the attention of hundreds of thousands has been drawn to the work; and many tens of thousands have come to see it. All this leads me to desire further and further to labor on in this way, in order to bring yet greater glory to the Name of the Lord. *That He may be looked at, magnified, admired, trusted in,* relied on at all times is my aim in this service; and so particularly in this intended enlargement. That it may be seen how much one poor man, simply by trusting in God, can bring about by prayer; and that thus other children of God may be led to carry on the work of God in dependence upon Him; and that children of God may be led increasingly to trust in Him in their individual positions and circumstances, therefore I am led to this further enlargement."

PRAYER AND TRUST IN GOD

The final point which I emphasize from Mr. Muller's narrative is the lesson of firm and unwavering trust in God's promise as the secret of persevering prayer. If once we have, in submission to the teaching of the Spirit in the Word, taken hold of God's promise, and believed that the Father has heard us, we must not allow ourselves by any delay or unfavorable appearances to be shaken in our faith.

"The full answer to my daily prayers was far from being realized; yet there was abundant encouragement granted by the Lord, to continue in prayer. But suppose, even, that far less had come in than was received, still, after having come to the conclusion, upon scriptural grounds, after much prayer and self-examination, I ought to have gone on without wavering, in the exercise of faith and patience concerning this object; and thus all the children of God, when once satisfied that anything which they bring before God in prayer, is according to His will, ought to continue in believing, expecting, persevering prayer until the blessing is granted."

"Thus am I myself now waiting upon God for certain blessings, for which I have daily besought Him for ten years and six months without one day's intermission. Still the full answer is not yet given concerning the conversion of certain individuals, though in the meantime I have received many thousands of answers to prayer. I have also prayed daily without intermission for the conversion of other individuals about ten years, for others six or seven years, for others from three or two years; and still the answer is not yet granted concerning those persons, while in the meantime many thousands of my prayers have been answered, and also souls converted, for whom I had been praying. I lay particular stress on this for the benefit of those who may suppose that I need only to ask of God, and receive at once; or that I might pray concerning anything, and the answer would surely come.

"One can only expect to obtain answers to prayers which are according to the mind of God; and even then, patience and faith may be exercised for many years, even as mine are exercised, in the matter to which I have referred; and yet am I daily continuing in prayer, and expecting the answer, and so surely expecting the answer that I have often thanked God that He will surely give it, though now for nineteen years faith and patience have thus been exercised. Be encouraged, dear Christians, with fresh earnestness to give yourselves to prayer, if you can only be sure that you ask things which are for the glory of God.

"But the most remarkable point is this, the funds from Scotland supplied me, as far as can be known now, with all the means necessary for fitting up and promoting the new orphan houses. Six years and eight months I have been day by day, and generally several times daily, asking the Lord to give me the needed means for this enlargement of the orphan work, which, according to calculations made in the spring of 1861, appeared to be about fifty thousand pounds, but which at a later period was found to be about fifty-eight thousand pounds: the total of this amount I had now received. I praise and magnify the Lord for putting this enlargement of the work into my heart, and for giving me courage and faith for it; and above all, for sustaining my faith day by day without wavering. When the last portion of the money was received, I was no more assured concerning the whole, than I was at the time I had not received one single donation towards this large sum. I was at the beginning, after once having ascertained His mind, through most patient and heart-searching waiting upon God, as fully assured that He would bring it about, as if the two houses, with their hundreds of orphans occupying them, had been already before me.

"I make a few remarks here for the sake of young believers in connection with this subject: 1.) Be slow to take new steps in the Lord's service, or in your business, or in your families: weigh everything well; weigh all in the light of the Holy Scriptures and in the fear of God. 2.) Seek to have no will of your own, in order to ascertain the mind of God, regarding any steps you propose taking, so that you can honestly say you are willing to do the will of God, if He will only please to instruct you. 3.) But when you have found out what the will of God is, seek for His help, and seek it earnestly, perseveringly, patiently, believingly, expectantly; and you will surely in His own time and way obtain it.

"To suppose that we have difficulty about money only would be a mistake: there occur hundreds of other wants and of other difficulties. It is a rare thing that a day occurs without some difficulty or some want; but often there are many difficulties and many wants to be met and overcome the same day. All these are met by prayer and faith, our universal remedy; and we have never been confounded. Patient, persevering, believing prayer, offered up to God, in the Name of the Lord Jesus, has always, sooner or later, brought the blessing. I do not despair, by God's grace, of obtaining any blessing, provided I can be sure it would be for any real good, and for the glory of God."

[1]The extracts are from a work in four volumes, *The Lord's Dealings with George Muller.* —Nisbet & Co., London.